The Naked Shoe:
The Artistry of Mabel Julianelli

The Naked Shoe:
The Artistry of Mabel Julianelli

Jane Julianelli

Previous page: Mabel Winkel works in her
Brooklyn studio, 1940.

ISBN 978 1 85149 639 6

British Library Cataloguing-in-Publication Data
A catalogue record for this book is available
from the British Library

Publication designed and typeset by
John and Orna Designs, London

Original photography by John Manno

Printed in the UK by Empress Litho

ACC Editions.
An imprint of
Antique Collectors' Club Ltd.,
Woodbridge, Suffolk, IP12 4SD

Contents

Acknowledgements

Thank you to: Harold Koda, Cassandra Gero, Suzanne Shapiro, Kristen Stewart, Elizabeth Bryan, Jessica Regan, Karin Willis, Joyce Fung, Meghan Lee at The Costume Institute of The Metropolitan Museum of Art; Michelle Harvey, MacKenzie Bennett, and Jennifer Schauer at The Museum of Modern Art; Leigh Montville, Shawn Waldron, Gretchen Fenston, Dawn Lucas, Alex Navissi, Cynthia Cathcart, Florence Palomo at Condé Nast; Kristina O'Neill, Lisa Luna, Juwon Ajayi at Harper's Bazaar; Simon Collins, June Weir, Howard Davis at Parsons The New School For Design; Valerie Steele, Patricia Mears, Colleen Hill, Ann Coppinger, Eileen Costa and Varounny Chanthasiri at Fashion Institute of Technology; Rebeccah Pailes-Friedman, Ashley M. Berger at Pratt Institute; Saks Fifth Avenue; Lord & Taylor; Diana Hoover at Lord & Taylor; John Manno; The Brearley School; The Richard Avedon Foundation; Eli and Phyllis Footer; Gerald Blum; John Schumacher; Lisa K. Digernes and Kenneth N. Swezey at Cowan, DeBaets, Abrahams & Sheppard LLP; Bernard Green; Diana Steel, John Brancati, Anna Morton, Lisanne Beretta, Sudha d'Unienville and Elizabeth Choi at Antique Collectors' Club Ltd; John and Orna Designs; Ken Simon; Tom Clavin; Jennifer Unter; the fabulous vintage fashion sellers who sent me great stories about loved-ones who wore Julianelli shoes, along with their shoes, included among others: Julie Gury of Joules Vintage, Desert Hot Springs, CA; Claudine Villardito of Black Cat Vintage, Tucson, AZ; Laura Brehmer of The Cats Pajamas, Williamsport, PA; Linda Davey of Loulou's Vintage, Sacramento, CA; Jonna Ellis of Tootsy's Treasures, Crestwood, KY; Elizabeth Scheinbart of The Vintage Mistress, Melbourne, FL; Iris and Steve Friedman; Florence Wildner; Ricki M. Perlowitz; Reba Sue Hurst; Sharon A. Reid; Vicki Sander; Johnny and Nancy Leyden; Ona and Jim Taranowski; Hal Jones; Phoebe Dunst; Stewart Kampel; Steve and Merlina Wakely; Michael Fried; Geoffry Fried; Stuart Berelson; Ashley Rebecca; Audrey and Gary Ferraro; Gina and Annabella; Patricia and Bird, Joe and Marian Stirrup; Jean McGowan; Onorata and Luigi Giulianelli; Esther and Charles Winkel; Annette and Jack Leyden; Jeanne and Joe Azzariti … and thank you, Mom and Daddy.

Next page: Forever a team, Mabel and Charles
in their Manhattan office, 1955.

To the wonderful Julianellis

Footnote to Fashion History:
Charles and Mabel Julianelli, perfectionists of the industry, are now designing and making their incomparable shoes for fine shops throughout the country.... Julianelli, 41 West 34th St. New York City

KALEIDOSCOPE OCTOBER 1948

259

Insignia, 1948.

Foreword

'Mabel Julianelli was a fiercely independent woman with great creative drive. Yet at the same time, she was a delightfully feminine woman who charmed the world with her grace and beautiful shoes.

The Mabel Julianelli book tells a marvelous story about love, life and a time when fashion was just beginning its magical adventure and designers dreamed of stardom with their names in brilliant lights. One of these dreamers was Mabel Julianelli, who came on the scene during the war years of the Forties and created shoe designs that destined her to become a Star. Her dynamic climb from a struggling Jewish childhood to become one of the first successful women to head her own corporation, Julianelli Inc., in the male dominated shoe business tells a story of this one-woman's struggle with grace and courage. I found it a story that simply inspired and delighted the soul.'

June Weir
Adjunct professor and lecturer at Parsons The New School For Design

Formerly: VP and Fashion Editor, *Women's Wear Daily* and '*W*' Magazine; Fashion News Director, *Vogue* Magazine; Deputy Style Editor, *New York Times* Sunday Magazine; Executive Editor, *Harper's Bazaar*; Contributing Editor, *Mirabella* Magazine

'At our very first meeting as we started talking about business I saw Mabel Julianelli's strength, her determination, that she was very bright. She was aware of what was happening around her and she had very strong instincts. Mabel, of all the people that I bought from, was the only one who had a complete fashion sense. In other words, the others only thought about the foot – she thought about the whole thing, and that gave me a feeling for her.

I was a shoe buyer at Lord & Taylor from 1965 to 1970. Basically all the other designers were more like manufacturers, and they had a designer and maybe the next year they'd get another designer.

There were a lot of very creative people in ready-to-wear, but not in shoes. Mabel was the creative person that I could relate to. She was for me a saving grace because she recognized my ability to understand fashion, not necessarily shoes, but that I understood how to put fashion together. I was one of those buyers who directed fashion, not just followed it. Also, if I gave her an idea about something she was far more receptive than the others were.

I had just become the buyer of shoes on the Fourth floor. With display, I always did a story. I wouldn't do anything without a story. Mabel did a low heel shoe with her fabulous bit buckle that was a hit at Lord & Taylor. We did it first in black patent leather and then we did it in everything. I would take that shoe, put it on a table in maybe five or eight colors, and that would be one story.

A lot of very good things came when I would be in Europe, Florence and Paris, twice a year with Mabel and we would go to the leather show. We stayed at the Plaza Athénée in Paris and the Grand in Florence or Excelsior. People like Newton Elkin or Palizzio would send their designer but they were not like Mabel, the top designer. I wanted to go with her because she was the only top designer and

Gerald Blum
Actor, innovator of fashion trends, former Executive Vice President of Lord & Taylor

she was the most creative. I went where the ideas came from and we had a lot of fun. Her peers were Ferragamo, Beth Levine, Newton Elkin.

But Mabel had a very strong feminine side to designing shoes and a strong point of view. Basically her shoes had class and I think that's the important factor.'

Howard Davis
Professor of Footwear Design,
Parsons The New School For Design

'I remember the first Julianelli shoe I saw; it was black and white and it had a bow in the back of the shoe at the top, and the bow tails hanging in back. I saw it at Jenny when I was working there, in Cincinnati Ohio. Mabel Julianelli did an ornament in back long before anyone else did it. It seemed like she knew the right last for the time, what was the last for now. I even remember how dramatic her name Julianelli was written in the shoe.

The thing that fascinated me most about Mabel Julianelli was how she connected the heel with the last. It was always like it was supposed to be. She knew how to put the last with the right heel and the heel with the right last, when to curve that heel in, or make it straight for it to be marketable.

To me she was always very contemporary. Her timing was good. She had her ear to the ground. She knew what was going to sell time-wise, and I think that was part of her success and her longevity. She knew how to edit a line of shoes which I thought was remarkable. It was very important to be able to edit that line for the consumer. She was always current; that attracted the consumer to her.

At Jenny, which carried Julianelli shoes, I was given Mabel's number and told I should meet her if I wanted to know how it was done. When I got to New York I called and she invited me to her sample room and office in the Marbridge Building, at Thirty-fourth Street and Sixth Avenue. She and Charlie showed me how the leather was hand-cut and pulled over the last and tacked underneath.

The Julianelli way to make a shoe is a lost art – that is, making a shoe from a sketch, paper pattern, and wooden last, which follows certain steps: Draw a design on the last, and from that make a paper pattern. Take your paper pattern to the cutting room where the pattern gets hand-cut. Tape your paper pattern or brass bound pattern after cutting. Go to pre-fitting where they mark where to put the bow, or tip, or overlay. Go to fitting where the shoe gets stitched together. Next to lasting, where the toe box is put in, then to the lasting machine, which grabs the leather and puts it over the last. Can you imagine anyone today taking the time to do all that for one shoe? When Mabel Julianelli was in business it was about quality; now it's quantity. They sold shoes against orders; now it's against sku's, which means stock keeping units or inventory.

I share with my students the artistry of Mabel Julianelli and I tell them, this is when people really cared.

Her feeling for color, feeling for mixing colors together was phenomenal. Her selection for lasts, the toe character, is it going to be round, single, double or triple needle point? She always knew how to fit that into a design. She also knew how to coordinate or mix that heel with that last and toe character. It was always there, to a point where I could look at a shoe and say, that's Julianelli.'

'There were a couple of people at that time that made shoes, for instance David Evins shoes, the I. Miller shoes, but Mabel's shoes were more sophisticated, more ladylike. She had more style and verve to the shoes than the other people. They were more fashionable and more creative than the others.

John Schumacher
Former president of I. Magnin & Company

We used to see her all the time. I met Mabel in Europe several times. She was terrific. She was very interesting, very helpful. Mabel's shoes were always ladylike, that was her look, the high heel shoes. She was involved in what was happening in fashion and clothes and how did these shoes interface with the clothes?

Charles was a shoe maker in the work room in the back, creating lasts. I think Mabel and Charles had a great relationship. She missed the creativity that he had and they had between them. He was the one that was doing a lot of this work in the back work room. I don't know how much of it was Charles and how much of it was Mabel, let's put it that way. He was very creative and I would go back and he would show me things that he was sketching on a last. They made exclusive shoes for people. I remember Charles showing me a last for Mrs. Vreeland.'

'I'll never forget—I climbed the Jungfrau in Julianelli shoes in the snow. Soaked as they were they were as good as new the next day. I didn't realize there would be snow but there we were, Steve, my husband and I, in Switzerland on the mountain, and I just kept going. I think the reason the shoes survived was because the hand-lasting of the leather was so superb.

I got to know Mabel after I married Steve. She wore a stunning black Ben Zuckerman suit to my wedding. She was lovely the first time I met her and Charles. I was taken by her elegance and her genuine sweetness.

Through the years we had great times. We would pick Mabel up on weekends and head out to Long Island. We'd get our dinner from the Sagg Store in Sagaponack. We would get their rotisserie chicken, coleslaw and corn pudding. And to us that was the perfect dinner.

She had excellent taste when it came to clothes and shoes. She had gone to Valentino when we were in Rome and loved Valentino. One year we traveled together, Mabel and Cousin Anne, Steve and I, to Athens and we cruised the Greek Islands. We had the most fun shopping, not knowing that Mabel was secretly a coin collector. She collected coins and wore them on chains, before it became a fad in New York."

Iris Friedman
Wife of Steve Friedman, Mabel's first cousin

'We were a very close family. I remember many Thanksgivings and Christmases spent in New York at their apartment.

Aunt Mabel always put her two hands on my head and kissed me each time she saw me. She was a loving aunt. I was special to her because I was Uncle Charles' flesh and blood. Everything was about her husband. I remember seeing her after Uncle Charles passed away. She was sitting in her living room, both arms hung down over the arms of the chair, and she said, "I'm very, very sad." I can't blame her, she idolized that man.'

John Charles Leyden
Mabel's nephew

'I loved them both! They were very cute and very warm to me. I met Mabel and Charles in 1960. They were hired to design for I. Miller. I started there as a shoe model in the late 1950s. I became the line builder for I. Miller, what is called a stylist today.

When I joined I. Miller, it was a group of designers, and none of it was really working. When they hired Mabel in 1960, it was a real coup; it was basically the first time a big-time designer worked for a big manufacturer.

One of the things that Mabel loved to do and she really was terrific at, was making bows and ornamentation. She was very well known for that, the door-knocker ornament, for instance.

My husband Eli Footer said Mabel was a great designer, and she was. Eli was at Schwartz & Benjamin and, while Mabel continued designing for I. Miller after I met her, she also designed a line for Schwartz & Benjamin in 1970. We remained friends for a long time. We had great times. When we weren't at the Chemin de Cuir leather show we shopped the flea markets in Paris together. I remember our giggle fits in the elevator of the Plaza Athénée.

Mabel introduced us to East Hampton. She loved it and I loved it. We went strawberry picking together in Watermill and then we made strawberry jam that day. It was a lot of fun. I really miss Mabel. She was a character. The Indian government invited Mabel to India to advise them, on what? I don't know, how to make shoes, how to work with leather, I don't know. All I know is that she did go and she bought a fabulous cabochon emerald ring there. You should wear it. You can wear it with jeans. She would!'

Phyllis Footer
Former Vice President of Schwartz & Benjamin

Part One
Mabel Winkel meets Charles Julianelli

Mabel felt comfortable in stiletto heels while riding the Balaganapati in New Delhi. After five o'clock open shank décolleté, called the Contessa, with scalloped tongue, tapered toe, needle-slim heel, 3⅝ inches, 1959. Photograph by John Manno.

March 9, 1959

Mabel Julianelli was seated in a howdah fourteen feet above the ground, atop one of the most carefully treated elephants in captivity, the Balaganapati. The elephant carried her along a mossy walking trail, fragranced with Hari champa vines, Cempaka telur Magnolias and Kadam trees. Several maharajas with their wives nodded to her along the elliptical Kewda bed. Mabel's short legs were splayed under a full shirtwaist.

   The carriage lay on a jeweled caparison and was harnessed by a wand of soft cords which fastened under the elephant's belly. This was the ride of the *fabulous* people — Jacqueline Kennedy and Lee Radziwill would take it a few years after Mabel. The challenge was to experience the great elephant's comportment of superiority and still hang on.

   Small, sparkling, shy and buxom. To look at her, one could never tell that shoe designer Mabel Julianelli was a big dream person, a fixed star, whose career in the capricious fashion business would last not just a few years, but four decades, because she was always one step ahead of it.

   Mabel made a pageant of the elephant ride; she wore white kid gloves, sunglasses, and a Hermès silk scarf tied under her chin as she crossed like a heavenly body over the Gandhrai Gardenia Park, behind New Delhi's lavish palace, the Ashoka Hotel, in the posh Chanakyapuri district.

   Remarkably, the animal did not object in any way to her presence aloft its spine, even acknowledged her sweetly with the ceremonious brandish of its rhinestone-speckled grey and pink trunk. The elephant was a very regal being because its imperial self-image had been reinforced by the Hindu system of reverence, elevating it to a position of sacredness, which was strictly enforced at that time.

"The Balaganapati recognizes a metaphysical self in your wife," said a soft-spoken handler to Mabel's husband and partner Charles Julianelli. Charles was dressed formally in a double-breasted suit, which Mabel told him to keep buttoned even in the Indian spring heat. "Your wife, she's a powerful lady," the handler commented.

At this time, the Ashoka Hotel hosted the most important guests in the world, including the Julianellis, who were in India to teach the craft of leather design.

Once deposited on the ground, Mabel wiggled her toes in her Julianelli shoes, happy to be lowered from a great height into their familiar, comfortable suspension, but unhappy to be once again shorter than everyone else.

Mabel was greeted by the royal spectators at the Ashoka Hotel, the maharajas and their maharinis. She noted that most of the women were wearing Julianelli shoes under their saris. It was one of the best days of her life.

"Be sure he gets caviar for dinner," said Mabel, stepping behind her husband's six-foot frame as she saw *Vogue* and *Paris Match* advancing at break-neck speed to interview her. Caviar might have sounded too frivolous, especially with the handler jumping in to inform her that elephants ate grass, roots, bark and branches. Then he told her that the Balaganapati was a girl. "Her name comes from one of our Hindu gods, Miss," he said, "it means beloved child."

"I was one of those," Mabel said, but she remembered how her father squeezed a pencil out of her little fingers and warned her that art was a distraction to the soul.

Manhattan! Fifth Avenue! Park Avenue! Thirty-Fourth Street! Forty-Second Street! These were not mere locations to Miss Mabel Winkel, looking from Brooklyn.

Mabel Winkel was the family mischief who made her father's heart race. She had been the child who came late, perhaps even a mistake. Her father reproached her for dreaming, yet dreaming made her who she was. Mabel blazed with a light of her own. She was allied to the stars by her imaginings. It would not be long before she was banging her little suitcase across the cobbled streets of Brooklyn toward the Bridge.

Mabel could have designed anything, and likely settled on shoes for the indisputable reason that, in 1926, SHOES HURT. At age seventeen, she must have wondered how she could run toward her future if the leather were hard and if she were expected to accept the Victorian notion – as many women still did – that painful corns and dislocated toes were fine as long as your feet looked petite.

Her mother's new shoes were never comfortable. Mabel always heard her say she'd 'break them in' and Mabel never forgot it. Years later, in a 1945 exhibition at the Museum of Modern Art in New York called 'Are Clothes Modern?', on the wall above the evolution of the shoe, a written motto expressed it perfectly:

The more helpless a woman, the more attractive she is supposed to be to man. To keep her from moving freely, he hampers her with anklets, stilts, hobbleskirts and heels.

In the same exhibition – in a room labeled 'Footwear without Tears' – were displayed two versions of the comfortable Julianelli Chopine sandal.

In the 1920s it was more than likely that a girl, growing up in the Russian immigrant section of Flatbush, Brooklyn, and a boy, growing up in the Italian-dominated Union City, New Jersey, would never meet. This is how it happened.

Esther (Essie), Mabel's mother, was one of six Jacobson sisters born to Simon, a push-cart peddler, and his wife Leah, who gave birth from Kentucky to New York, corner of Mulberry and Mott. Simon and Leah, both born around 1860 in Russia, came to America in their twenties, set up a hardware store, then moved their family from the Lower East Side to Flatbush, Brooklyn. Rural Brooklyn was lovely, but Mabel soon outgrew it.

Mabel Winkel for Mabel Winkel & Co. Sketches
showing buckles, bows and ornaments, 1938.
© 2010 Jane Julianelli.

The six Jewish sisters married Jews, their fifteen children married Jews, and their grandchildren married Jews. The Jacobsons married a Burger, a Kaminstein, a Robinson, a Pellman, a Winkel and a Friedman. Burger married a Levy and a Goldfeder. Kaminstein married a Kaplan and a Stein, Kaplan married a Diamond and a Roob.

The oddity was Miss Mabel Winkel who, being lost to any consideration of conformity, stunned her family of several hundred Jews by taking up one day, as cheerful as a bird, with a Roman Catholic Italian. It was then that Mabel Winkel learned the meaning of *shock value*. And it would stay with her.

In 1926, with money from her much older brother Ben, Mabel went to Pratt Institute and studied at the School of Fine and Applied Art in Costume Design. She had wanted to attend the School of Architecture but, having spent a lot of time staring up at the Ocean Parkway Jewish Center on Ditmas, and wondering why such a tall building didn't topple over, she decided a stiff neck wasn't worth it.

Mabel's father, Charles (Papa) Winkel, had a character consisting of a flighty nature, an intolerant mind, and a miserable temperament. She could never adjust herself to him, and they argued over every topic, especially her artistic inclination.

Papa Winkel was, like many, blown around by conflicting ideologies, attaching himself one year to the American Socialist Party, and the next year to capitalism in the form of real estate ventures. Mabel Winkel was similar to very few, with her own ideology; she was aware that there was beauty in the world and searched for a way to interpret it.

Her siblings were Jack the conformist, Ben the deal maker, and Helen the shy waif. All of them were born at least twenty years before Mabel, and had left home by the time she was growing up. Papa Winkel gave to each of them doses of his intolerance for any subject matter not favouring the Jews, yet it took his youngest child to see that he was not really a bigot, just a scared man. He was frightened of America, yet grateful at the same time that he and his family had never had to endure anti-Semitism in Europe. If he wasn't proselytizing, he was proselytizing. Mabel's talent for sketching outraged him. The topic of art in Papa Winkel's house was forbidden.

Always in a mad dash to be away from him, with paper and pencil in hand, Mabel worked her father into a state of frenzy. He called her a 'pipsqueak' because she was short and annoying. She, meanwhile, sketched everything that sparkled: her mother's jewelry, tokens of Papa Winkel's real estate wins, Essie's Egyptian-inspired jet bangles copied from the Pharaohs, and a flapper-inspired

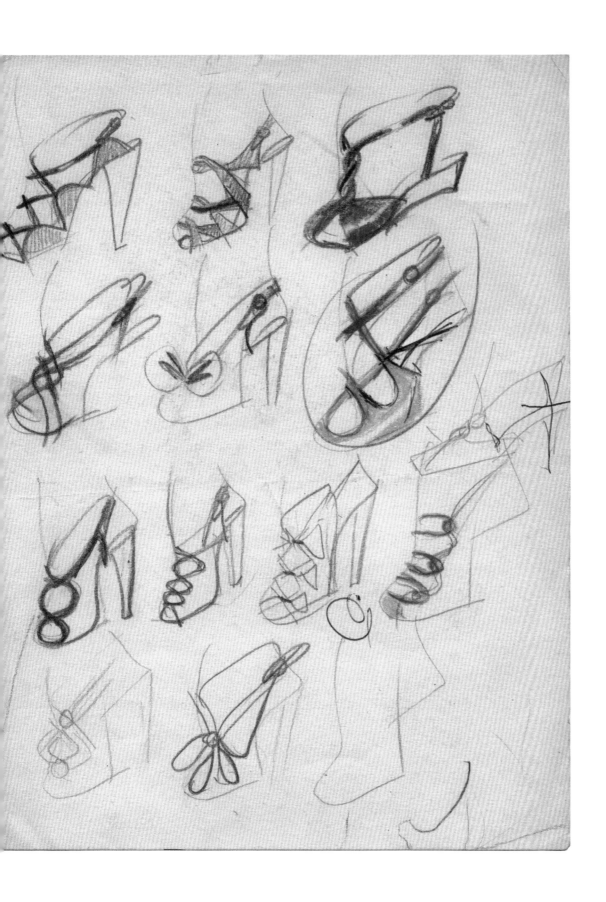

Mabel Winkel for Mabel Winkel & Co. Sketches including the earliest double-straps and t-straps, 1938. © 2010 Jane Julianelli.

crystal bead necklace that was set with onyx and citrine. They became little gems of fascination when she drew them on paper.

The sight of the flapper necklace was particularly memorable because of the way it clashed with her mother's character; this glittering object from the Roaring Twenties hung as low as Essie's breasts, screaming incongruity against her coarse serge skirt, wooly jersey and the cardboard-stiff garters that held up her Russian herringbone stockings. Mabel watched her mother tie the necklace in a rough knot so she wouldn't trip. She thought it was the most innovative thing Essie ever did, and wondered if rich women tied a knot in their pearls.

It was a miracle for Mabel to get out of that house, even if she did only make it four miles away to Pratt Institute.

Wonderful Pratt, its Armistice Day flagpole erected in the same year Mabel attended, at its base, the bronze busts of women symbolizing the arts, science and labor in honor of the men and women who served in World War I.

Mother Essie, who never left the shtetl, smelled like the guts of fish. She'd circle her kitchen table, flapping her wide arms and waving a cleaver with which she made the solyanka soup. Essie took in Russian and Polish Jewish immigrants who had fled the pogroms in Eastern Europe and Mabel remembered that Essie cooked for them and gave them cots when they passed out from tea and vodka. They would sleep it off in the hallways, the attic, and the basement.

Her parents were each in their own world: Papa Winkel, yelling clear to Ocean Parkway, in Russian, in Dutch, in Yiddish, cursing his youngest girl, "Look, my hand is shaking – I'm so mad at that pip-squeak!" he'd say, while Essie Winkel yelled back, "There is always a line at the bread vendor Wassily. But if you catch the eye of Gleb, ah, then, he'll get you in." It was just Mabel, her parents and the immigrants; her only solace was sketching.

At eighteen, Mabel Winkel, scared to death of the outside world beyond the shtetl, but armed with gigantic ambition and touched-up with a little fruit stain applied to her lips and cheekbones, walked into the Conaway-Winter Shoe Company of Washington Street, Brooklyn and interviewed for a job designing patterns for shoes. Conaway asked her, "Do you think you have shoe sense?" and she answered, "Shoe sense? You might tell Winter I have fashion sense."

Despite her generally reserved manner, Mabel had a striking effect in the factory. Conaway would say she designed patterns that "come out of the clouds", and she gained the attention of her co-workers for her talent. But they commented that she was shy. She tried to keep one of her attributes well-hidden, strapping her breasts to appear flat-chested which was the fashion. However, she conceded that she could not do it because it was painful beyond belief, and seemed a bit tasteless. Mabel wore felt cloches from which she removed anything which she did not make herself, such as bows, knots, tassels and ribbons, deeming them unworthy of her personal style. She peered out from under them with huge dark, liquid eyes. The only feature she possessed that seemed to have bones was her hair – a wiry golden brown mass that had started out as blond baby curls, which even a cloche couldn't tame. On her feet Mabel wore stiff black leather high-tops with wooden buttons up the side. She was still in uncomfortable shoes, but her step burst unrestrained. Her eyes were wild to break away.

Charles Julianelli for Mabel Winkel & Co. Original paper pattern of the two-strap anklet, black suede, hidden closure, 1941.

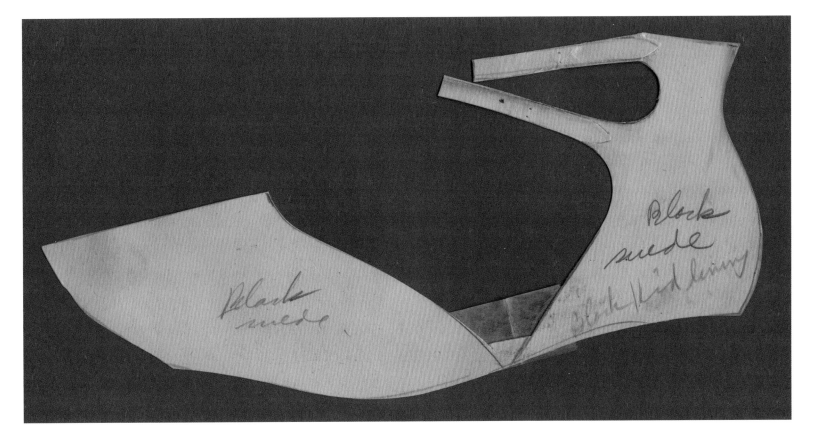

Carlo Aldo Giulianelli was born in Lucca, Italy, in 1907. By the age of twenty he was learning the technical end of the business in the same factory as Mabel Winkel, converting designs into patterns which he measured on hard paper with his calipers and micrometers.

1927 was the year of the Dempsey-Tunney rematch in Chicago and Calvin Coolidge was president. Charles attended The Cooper Union in New York, took free-hand drawing classes, and wrote down 'shoe designer' as his occupation. He started his love affair with America, a child immigrating to America from Italy, seeing it for the first time as a boy of four. He grew up wanting to be an instant American.

Charles intended to exercise the same Americanization over his given name, Carlo Aldo, as he did over his whole being. He was the only member of the family to keep the American name, Charles, given to him by the immigration officials at Ellis Island. They had also changed the other family names: his mother, Onorata, became Nora; his father, Luigi, became Louis; and his sister, Annetta, became Annette. Charles was also the only one who kept the American officials' spelling change of his surname, Giulianelli to Julianelli, even though the letter 'J' did not exist in the Italian alphabet.

Homesick for her Renaissance-walled town of Lucca in Tuscany, mother Onorata would not change her name, signing Giulianelli to the daily letters she sent home. However, the advantage for her son did not escape her, and with a wave of her rosary beads and a look cast toward the ceiling, she blessed their new land and left her only son free to be Charles Julianelli.

Onorata Giulianelli (née Nardi) was pious, romantic, strong-willed, blond and blue-eyed. She brought her children across the Atlantic Ocean, standing them on the deck of the ship and reading to them in Italian from a little booklet, the writings of St Catherine of Sienna, 'Everything comes from love,' she read. 'All is ordained for the salvation of man,' she continued when they landed at Ellis Island, and on the dock in New York Harbor, 'God does nothing without His goal in mind'. When she saw her husband, Luigi, waiting for them she stopped reading. They had made it, thanks to St Catherine.

Luigi was the right sort of man to be a trailblazer – massive, stern and a bit scary. He rented a flat for the family under New York's Sixth Avenue elevated railway (El) and made spaghetti in a little Italian joint on Ninth Avenue. The children were beautiful, dark haired like Luigi and with the graceful features of Onorata. From the moment she landed until the day she died, Onorata called them all by their Italian names: Aldo (Charles' middle name), Annetta, and the youngest, Eugenia, who was born in New York. Onorata Giulianelli was very hard put to find comfort in her new city, and she begged Luigi to move the family to the New Jersey suburbs and fingered her rosary beads in the gloom of the El until he did.

Charles, the acknowledged jewel of the family, was better looking than the cinema star, Rudolph Valentino, with a square masculine face, a wedge of thick black hair, and most prominent, elegant eyebrows that pointed to the many dreams waiting inside his head.

He wanted to make his fortune as a portrait artist.

He posed for an art class and had an exquisite body, as students who sketched him at The Cooper Union would bear out, but he showed no conceit, and was very popular. He soon came to be known as a kind-hearted man.

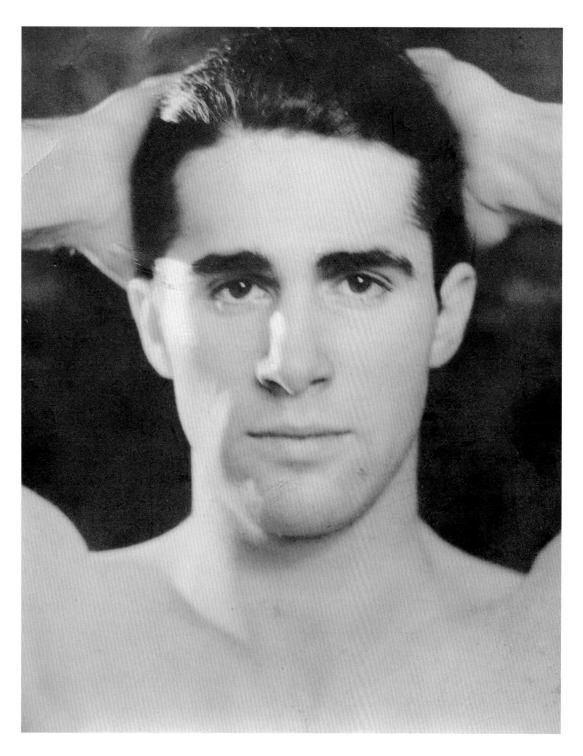

Charles as a drawing class model
at The Cooper Union, 1928.

Charles in his painter's smock, 1927.

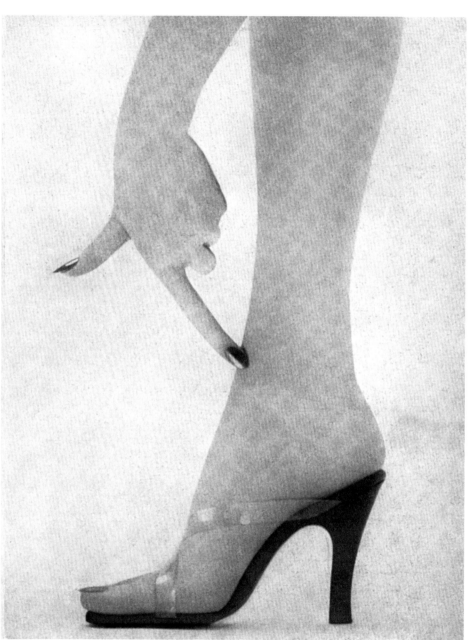

The Julianelli Mule

Top left: Dye-able straw mule, 1948. As seen in US *Harper's Bazaar.*

Bottom left: Back interest on a mule's black velvet spike heel, a triangular blaze of rhinestones, 1950. As seen in US *Harper's Bazaar.*

Above: Mule with plastic straps, 1952. As seen in US *Harper's Bazaar.*

Soft band mule, asymmetrical in white, heel: 3⅝ inches, seen in Monaco, 1960. Photograph by John Manno.

Opposite: Slip-on evening mule with asymmetrical banding showing Mabel's talent with architectural construction: it is statuesque and completely in balance. To be worn making an entrance down a long staircase at a black tie event, heel: 3½ inches, 1970. Photograph by John Manno.

This page: Wide-band sandal-mule, tapered stack wood heel: 3 inches, 1970. Photograph by John Manno.

Mabel and Charles meet

On the day Mabel and Charles were introduced at work, Mabel walked toward him, her big brown eyes dropped demurely, her hand extended and her pace unsteady, as if she herself were crossing the Atlantic. For the second time, the first being Pratt, she thought that something wonderful was about to happen. Of Mabel, Charles could have only one first impression – a tiny package of buxom beneficence.

Mabel and Charles both worked in the drab, rubber-cement-scented Brooklyn factory of Conaway-Winter-Ochs, and sat at grey metal desks lit by flexi-lamps, with grey metal stems and rotating grey metal shades. Mabel sketched and Charles measured and cut models, both looking up from time to time in the direction of the other. Before long their ambition brought them together.

Conaway and Winter chatted among themselves, fearing they might lose the two soon. When they sent them to their Boston factory, their partner, Ochs commented: "We might lose the two soon."

Charles and Mabel both lived with their parents; Charles was at 317 Twelfth Street in Union City, New Jersey, eleven miles from Mabel at 570 East Eighth Street in Brooklyn. Back then, there was little access to the telephone, and no e-mail or texting.

Behind the strange little woman who wore her skirt long and her cloche low, Charles saw that Mabel was pretty.

She was not a conventional beauty, but had a kind of prettiness that came from being brashly American.

And so he wrote her letters, dozens of them.

During the summer vacation of 1928, Mabel went to the neighborhood movie theater with her older sister Helen. Mabel's knowledge of glamour was limited to the movie queens, Greta Garbo and Jean Harlow. In the evening, the stifling Flatbush air brushed over Mabel's face. She could hear her father pounding his fist on the kitchen table downstairs. From her room Mabel followed Charles' lighthearted handwriting rolling across the pages of his letters, describing in cheery detail playing the violin, going for hayrides in Pompton Lakes with *Mercedes*, sharing birthday cake and wine with *Anna*, and watching movies at the Strand with *Elena*, followed by ice cream at St Joseph's Bazaar.

He wrote to Mabel that his dream was to be a portrait painter; he had painted the Madonna and Child for his priest, a portrait of the Mayor of Union City, and a likeness of Charles Lindbergh which was so good that Lindbergh's mother wanted it. As Charles listened to the Dempsey-Tunney fight he worked until 3 am on his portrait of President Coolidge, which he planned to take to Washington D.C.

"Why can't I have his life," Mabel railed, "so clean-cut American?"

The next summer, in 1929, Charles had narrowed it down to one girl – *Elena* – from Villa Geneva in Pennsylvania's Mt. Pocono, where he and his sister Annette were vacationing. 'I'm with Elena and Annette in the fresh cool breeze, motoring, swimming and dancing ... playing my violin to Elena's piano,' he wrote, and Mabel got antsy.

Mabel crumpled up his letter. It was the last 'summertime fun' letter from him she would endure. She saw she was dealing with an adorable adolescent who hadn't wised up yet. A plan hatched.

"I want to speak face to face," she said to Charles in the late summer of 1929, what turned out to be a precarious time for business. Mabel was twenty years old. She asked Charles to go into partnership with her in a design business she would call Mabel Winkel & Co. He said yes.

"The Julianellis had their shoes made at the Zuckerman & Fox factory downtown in New York City. That was in the day when there were thirty-six factories in New York making shoes. People from Europe would come to us to have their shoes made. For instance, a shoe, say from Paris, with leather draped over the last form would be sent to a New York factory, accompanied by sketch, pattern and pullover.

Today it's so different. The manufacturing is done in China and Brazil. And where do people get their designs? There are design teams or design companies; you go to them and you buy a design. Someone sits in front of a computer and messes around with it, which I think shows no craftsmanship whatsoever. Few designers today know how to construct a shoe, or know pattern making.

In the old days it was called bench-making when the cobbler would sit at a bench and tack the upper, which is the leather piece before it is attached to the shoe, in other words, the top of the shoe. The cobbler would drop the upper on the shoe form. That's the original way.

He would handset the shank with sawdust and glue. That was called hand setting a shank by packing. Today the shank is incorporated into the insole."

Howard Davis
Professor of Footwear Design,
Parsons The New School For
Design.

They courted in secret, and never in the beautiful
Brooklyn of Mabel's youth. Courting 1938.

Opposite: Slit-cut sling, stack wood heel:
3½ inches, 1960. Photograph by John Manno.
This page: Delicate V-strap sling, heel: 3¼ inches,
late 1970. Photograph by John Manno.

Together in business

It was another damp studio in Brooklyn, but this time it was theirs: one room for the showroom and a cubby-hole sample factory. Charles in a smock, worked in the back with a timid, sad-eyed Italian pattern-maker, Vincent Greco, whom Mabel hired to help Charles. The two men rarely left the cubbyhole and sang Italian lullabies all day, until Mabel put a stop to it and the men limited themselves to humming. At eighteen years old, Vincent's hair was completely grey, brought on, Mabel deduced, by the way he worried.

The new little business ran just the same as when the Julianellis worked for the pattern company. The samples went out to the manufacturers as Mabel Winkel & Co., just the same. In 1934, Charles became a United States citizen at the Courts of Common Pleas, Jersey City. During the demise of hundreds of manufacturers in the early 1930s and a lot of heated criticism coming from Flatbush over her 'reckless endangerment of a nice Italian boy',

Mabel and Mabel Winkel & Co. pranced ahead confidently, despite the Stock Market Crash and her father's opinion.

Mabel created the shoe with the understanding of an architect, its functional and aesthetic structure, composition, balance and compatibility of parts, but she researched it like a typical movie-crazed schoolgirl. Her designs could have taken any form, a building, a sculpture, or a painting, because her shoes would later be compared to all of these. When it came to inspiration she went to the movies.

Judy Garland, Joan Crawford and the costume designer, Adrian, who dressed them, were in her sites through the 1930s. Later it would be Katharine Hepburn and the formidable American designer, Charles James. But mostly, it took a movie queen like Carole Lombard – *My Man Godfrey* was out that year – whose body floated in her clothes, to inspire Mabel's collection of the I Thee Wed Slipper in 1936, a lithe white sandal, tied at the ankle with soft satin ribbons done in peach, in powder blue, in chartreuse, in rose, in blush.

Charles and Vincent chuckled over the samples. "You'd better marry her," kidded Vincent.

Bergdorf Goodman liked the slippers so much that they showed them with their Miss Bergdorf collection, as well as in their incomparable shoe salon. Arnold Constable also wanted the slippers, but stores at that time demanded exclusives, so Mabel & Co. gave them instead a high heel that

Opposite: Mabel brought her 'I Thee Wed' evening sandal inspiration of 1936 to Saks Fifth Avenue in 1947. Unknown source.

laced up the front in grey gabardine with grey patent trim. Arnold Constable loved it so much that they put the shoe in their New Rochelle branch which had just opened.

Mabel made circle ornaments on a pump, and encrusted rhinestones on the circle. Sometimes she'd partially hide it with a bow. It became one of many signature designs. Other early signatures were a two color mix, such as red and white straps for the Tailored Woman, or a gold kid and white satin weave. If she said 'no' to bows it was because something in nature attracted her.

Then Mabel flipped the last around to the back, designing what she called, a 'back interest', with a bow, ornament or rhinestones attached to the heel. Charles and Vincent looked at each other.

"You'd better talk to her," Vincent warned Charles in Italian, "she's designing on the wrong end."

Years later, in 1948, Mabel named that shoe the Backswept. She enjoyed their alarm, watching them get nervous in her mischievous way, and when it was almost on Charles' lips to bring up the subject of Mabel's imagination, she presented him with an extravagant upper on a wood last that carried such a huge bow high on the vamp, that the last disappeared behind it. Her inspirations were the enormous wide brimmed hats designed by Madame Paulette and Lily Daché.

"The foot's gone," Vincent whispered to Charles in a panic.

"She knows what she's doing," Charles calmed him. And he was right. The 1939 design was so popular that it was adapted for 1940 spring wear.

There was no stopping her. Known as the 'Number One Shoe Designer for Women', Mabel Winkel became the wonder child of 1940 with a slew of designs, each embodying a first-time construction, a first-time comfort level, a first-time aesthetic. She covered the foot like a torso, with attention to every part. She designed a vamp-shortening upper treatment, a sturdier arch support, a patented flexible grained kidskin sport shoe, and a two-shade open-toe pump.

Mabel's ideal street shoe was a spectator pump with wedge heel and V-throat in leather and linen. She perforated a suede wedge, gave shock value to the heel with a back interest, designed a reveal of open toe that put the peep-toe of the day to shame, and most of all, made every woman want to dance in her sandals. It was the beginning of the world's love affair with Mabel's sandals – bare, dancing sandals, the first ones, in gold and silver, or patriotic red, white and blue.

The *Philadelphia Inquirer* in October 1941, unable to think up any descriptive phrase that remotely did justice to a Mabel shoe, compared it to fine porcelain or rare carving. 'We have been creating

Mabel Julianelli for Mabel Winkel & Co.
Sketches of ankle treatments and t-straps, 1940.
© 2010 Jane Julianelli.

1 A striped evening gown inspired Mabel to make this sketch, the first step in making a new slipper. At top are pullovers of other new slippers.

2 Next Mabel pencils her design on a wooden last, or foot model. A design that's attractive on paper may be an utter failure on the foot.

3 Mabel takes the penciled last to a skilled workman in her little shoe factory and watches him closely as he cuts a pattern of her design. From this pattern he will cut the leather or fabric for the pullover which will be tacked down on the wooden last.

Mabel Winkel

NUMBER ONE

SHOE DESIGNER FOR WOMEN

MABEL WINKEL is known as the wonder child of the shoe designing field. She deserves the title. Only a little more than a decade ago, she was an unknown art student at Pratt Institute in Brooklyn. Today she is one of America's foremost designers of fashionable footwear and millions of women wear her creations.

Miss Winkel, who is only 30, rose to success on the wings of one practical idea. When she set up shop as a designer, most American shoe artists simply sold the sketches of their designs to manufacturers. Mabel decided to go a step further and see how her ideas would work out in leather before she tried to sell them.

With the co-operation of Charles Julianelli, her husband and partner, she set up a tiny factory and commissioned skilled shoemakers to work out her designs. Then, when she actually had "pullovers" to show—a pullover is the upper part of a shoe minus sole and heel—she went to the manufacturers.

They bought and have been buying ever since. Today Miss Winkel has yearly contracts with some of the best known firms in the shoe-manufacturing business.

Because shoe lines are shown and sold three to six months before other lines—dresses, coats, gloves or hats —Mabel Winkel must be a prophet as well as an artist.

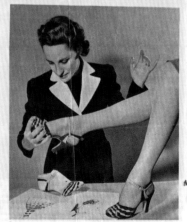

4 Mabel compares the finished slipper manufactured by her client with her pullover (on the table) and the sketch of the striped dress.

40

An article from 1940 describing the intricacies of Mabel Winkel's creative process, citing her as the 'number one shoe designer for women'. Unknown source.

GRAINED KIDSKIN SPORT SHOE is so unusual that Mabel obtained a pat-
on it (she has several construction and design patents). It is very flexible,
gives excellent support. Mabel designed it for a big department store.

MABEL WINKEL'S 1940 FASHION FOOTNOTES

OPEN-TOE PUMP, in two shades of
own, is Mabel's "ideal street shoe."

A SPECTATOR PUMP, with wedge heel
and V-throat, in leather and linen.

PERFORATED SUEDE, whose broad
rap is only for girls with slim ankles.

A RED, WHITE AND BLUE evening sandal follows the popular patriotic note.

MABEL WINKEL ... continued

SHE WALKS IN BEAUTY—
AND IN COMFORT, TOO!

SMART COMFORT FOR OFFICE

MABEL WINKEL DESIGNED THIS PUMP to increase the
efficiency of an efficient secretary. Of soft calf and
buckskin in two shades of brown, it has a sturdy arch
support, firm heel, vamp-shortening design.

AFTERNOON PUMP with
several fashion highlights:
open toe; back interest (a
bow on heel); V-throat;
two colors (brown and
tan); two kinds of leather
(calfskin and suede).

ELEGANT FOR EVENING

CLIENTS LIKED this 1939 design
so well that Mabel is adapting
it for 1940 wear in spring materials and colors. The large buck-
le-bow does wonders to give the
impression of a short vamp,
therefore a shorter, smaller foot.

"Today, instead of hand-making the way it used to be, the process is computerized. Shoes today are made for speed. Even the lasts have changed. When I came into the industry the lasts were wood. Now today they're plastic. It used to be when they made a last it would be hand-turned on a lathe. Now you put it in a computer, press buttons and a plastic last shoots out. The uppers are computerized too, as far as how the design is done."

Howard Davis
Professor of Footwear Design,
Parsons The New School For
Design.

shoes you'd have to see to believe,' said Mabel in *Footnotes*, 'and you can see them in the stores; even then you'd probably suspect you were dreaming. They are gay, witty, sometimes eccentric, always exciting.'

Vincent raised his eyes to the ceiling. "Watch out, she's coming in with more crazy ideas," he said.

Every part of the process was hand-made or bench made. Mabel sketched her design on paper first, then penciled the design on a wood last, which she gave to Charles and Vincent, and from the pattern they cut the leather or fabric pullover, and tacked the pullover over the wood last.

Mabel stayed mostly in the background where she felt more comfortable and when buyers came to their studio, Charles spoke to them, coaxing them to follow Mabel's instinct, instead of their own, while Mabel buried her head in a book about Greek or Medieval footwear. She intuitively knew how to handle the business, what kind of contacts should be made, what kind of contracts should be signed. She could dress Charles and teach him how to speak to financial people and how to entertain fashion people.

To go to work, Mabel calmed her brown hair in a wave, wore navy or black full skirts, hemmed below the knee, and dark, loose unrevealing blouses raised high on the neck, topped by a choker of tiny beads. She put slender Charles in charcoal grey tapered double-breasted suits with broad lapels to show off his physique.

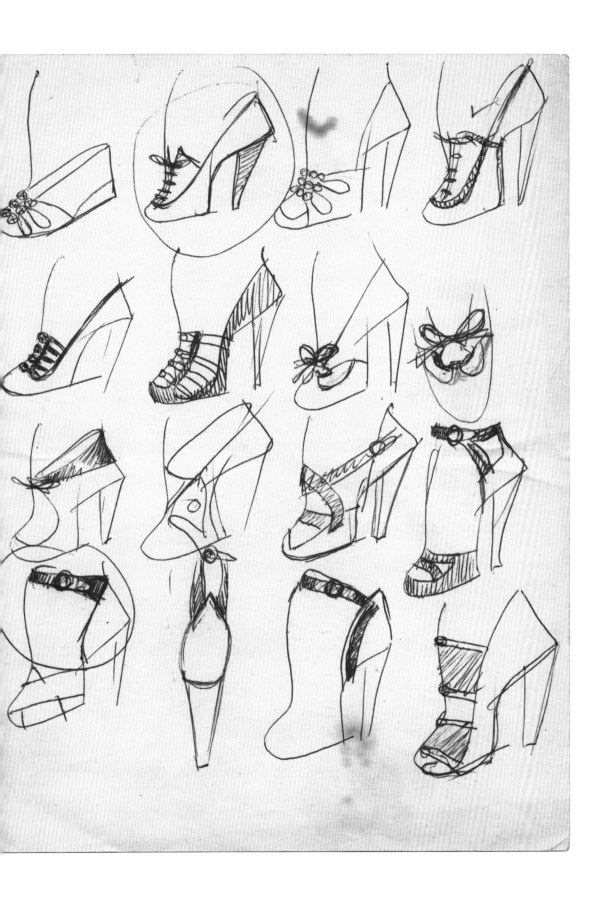

Mabel Winkel for Mabel Winkel & Co. Sketches, showing her earliest wedge, Baroque, lace-ups (first row), V-throat (third row) and back interest (fourth row), 1939. © 2010 Jane Julianelli.

Mabel and Charles each still lived with their parents. The Julianellis had moved to the second floor of a two-family house at 570 Fortieth Street in North Bergen, with Aunt Katie, Onorata's sister, and Uncle Alfred Gemignano downstairs. Mabel and Charles were rarely seen in public together, never in Flatbush. Once in a while Charles took Mabel to Jersey for a movie at the Strand followed by ice cream at St Joseph's Bazaar. In some ways, they were still children acting grown-up. They had gone straight to work in their teens, and in their twenties were following the dictates of their separate religions. No socializing was the custom for Jew and Catholic. Mabel and Charles worked all day together, then said good night and went home.

"There seems to be something new about you, Charles," observed his sister Annette, sweet, pretty and perceptive. "Are you in love?" It seemed impossible, but with his thoughts of fun and creativity at the studio, sharing everything with Mabel as a team, designing everything new, and the crazy innovations with which they were enlightening American manufacturers, it seemed to Charles that he also felt new, more light-hearted, and happier, because someone very precious had his back.

Mabel, in the course of time, prolonging their courtship for the sake of keeping everybody happy hoped with all her heart that Charles would not turn out to be so wonderful, that she would find at least one tiny flaw in him and not succumb to any romantic feelings. But how could she not?

He was fair, honest, loving, smart and gentle. Worse still, he was gorgeous.

Also, he relieved her of the task of handling the money because he was good with numbers. Another dismal fact was his perfect compatibility with Mabel in the brains and talent departments – both thought the other was more creative. If all that weren't enough, he was a family man, and if anyone could get the two families to love them as a couple, he could. Charles was a breed of man Mabel had never known. Just as Glenn Miller's band played in 1939, they were both definitely 'In the Mood'.

Mabel asked her mother, "What does this word Jewish mean? Is it like tallish? Does it mean I'm sort of a Jew?"

Essie gasped at her irreverent daughter. Nobody before had questioned it.

"Either I'm a Jew," said Mabel, "or I'm not."

Mabel Julianelli for Mabel Winkel & Co.
Sketches including t-straps, ankle-straps
and beaded overlay embellishment, 1940.
© 2010 Jane Julianelli.

Essie assured Mabel she was one-hundred per cent Jew and

no one she married but a Jew would fit into their family of many Jews.

"How could you even work with a *Jewess*?" Elena, a beautiful girl of Italian descent, spit the word at Charles. They were in a recital hall playing a duet. Elena's womanly intuition had been alerted recently and she surmised that Charles and Mabel weren't just working buddies. She turned abruptly on her piano bench, right in the middle of Strauss's Blue Danube Waltz. "You know what they say about them – they're too clever for their own good."

"Mabel is a Jew," Charles said, "but Catholic, Jew, Italian, Russian, we are all Americans here. I'll tell you something, no one is like Mabel."

One evening Mabel and Charles went to the Penny Bridge at Newtown Creek on the Brooklyn side. The moon was just about to fall off the triangular wooden frame and disappear behind a fringe of clouds, but Mabel could see Charles all the same, standing a few feet from her, then approaching until he was kissing her and she was in his arms. Mabel was thinking, besides the warmth of it, that he was a pro at this, with many girls like her, on many bridges like the Penny Bridge, in many moonlights. Difficult though the kiss had been to acquire, once she had it, she never let it go. It would be a miserable existence for them, she thought, and the end of their business if they didn't marry now. Sitting down on the bank, they talked about their parents until the moon was gone.

"My father wouldn't like it," said Charles. "I don't think he's ever smiled at a single thing I've done. One time he did, when Annette and I were squashing the grapes. We were covered in red grape juice from the barrel that Pop and Uncle Alfred put on the table to make Pop's wine."

"Do you think your Pop only smiled because you were a big red blob?" asked Mabel who had been to Charles' house and saw how distant Luigi was, so unlike Onorata, who adored her son.

"No, I just think he was happy because we kids made wine for him," Charles laughed.

"My Papa always scowls at me," said Mabel, "I mean, after my brothers and my sister, I'm a bit of a disappointment."

Mabel and Charles were bound together by ambition and their differences did not matter; she hid in shadow, he thrived in light; he liked people, conversation, flirting, while she was more reserved, depending on him to deal with the world for her.

Mabel Julianelli for Mabel Winkel & Co. Sketches including modified t-straps (left), wedges (right top), lace up and ribbon anklets (right), 1940. © 2010 Jane Julianelli.

The dancing slings in patriotic red and blue kicked up their heels at the USO Clubs during the 1940s, and at Roseland Ballroom in the 1950s. Dancing heel: 3¾ inches. Photograph by John Manno.

Eleanor Lambert told the Julianellis at Henri Soulé's Le Pavillon, "An ornament can express designing genius." Mabel called it The Mae West. Overlay embellishment, a triple semi-ring of pearls and blue beads on a halter sling, mezzanine heel: 3½ inches, late 1940. Photograph by John Manno.

She was curious how life would be without her Jewish surname Winkel, if it were ever mercifully replaced by the beautiful – exotic – Tuscan vineyards – verdant hills – and sensual nights of *Julianelli*. Wisely, Charles Julianelli had stuck to a spelling that made Julianelli easy for Americans to pronounce.

The evening became suddenly warmer. A rowboat moved through the pilings of the Penny Bridge. Charles gave Mabel a playful, sideways glance, raising one amused eyebrow. "Aren't we the most fortunate two kids that ever lived? Do you think we're falling in love?"

"How do you know when you're in love?" asked Mabel.

"Your chest hurts, and you're sick to your stomach."

"That's not love; that's an appendicitis. But maybe I'm in love," she answered.

"There are no maybes in the human heart," he said playfully, offering her his lifted eyebrow, which somewhat lifted her fears about how the world would receive them as a couple.

It was an awful thing to happen, but the account of Elena's suicide, during their courtship in 1938, stayed with Mabel and Charles for a long time after they were married. Charles had started seeing Mabel after calling it quits with his previous girlfriend Elena. The concept of marrying Elena had been as implausible an idea to Charles as any he could imagine, even though she lived next door to him in Jersey and was an Italian Roman Catholic; even though she vacationed with her parents in Mt. Pocono and went hay riding with him at the Everson's Club in Pompton Lakes, and even though she played the piano to accompany his violin.

Elena jumped out of a window onto Fortieth Street in Union City. Uncle Alfred and Aunt Katie came running down from upstairs. Elena's father came over the next day to tell Onorata and Luigi Elena's last words: she was sorry she couldn't have Charles, but she wasn't as clever as the Jewess.

Onorata spoke to Charles later in Italian: "Unfortunate girl, she gave up her life, not for love, but for hate." They were words from the writings of St Catherine of Sienna.

December, 1939. So deeply involved were Mabel and Charles in the struggle of merging their talents, they ceased to notice the events that shaped their lives.

Just a week before Thanksgiving in that year Mabel's mother Essie Winkel died. The funeral was held at Riverside Memorial Chapel in New York. Mabel took time off and didn't see Charles for a month.

A week before Christmas, Charles traveled by train from Jersey to take his sister Annette to see the decorations at Macy's. Annette believed things came in threes, like the Holy Trinity. Two events had never been more compelling in Charles' and Mabel's life: Elena's suicide and Essie's death, and Annette admonished Charles, if he planned to marry Mabel, to watch for a third, this one bound to be joyous.

"Oh, fratello mio," Annette screamed on Macy's main floor, "how glorious!"

"Look at the little chamber musical group!" Charles yelled.

"Look!" cried Annette, "Tinsel, gold wreaths – and Mabel?"

Charles looked up and saw Mabel at the top of the escalator, a tiny queen in navy, wearing a Tom Brigance coachman's cape. Charles waved wildly. Mabel, seeing Charles for the first time since her mother's funeral, paled to an almost inhuman whiteness. Tears of joy came to Charles' eyes, and Annette pretended nothing along the lines of victory for the Holy Trinity had occurred.

Charles was at the bottom of the escalator in a smart jacket and trousers, which Mabel had picked for him for the office, and a seasonal tie with Santa Clauses and reindeer, definitely not Mabel's choice.

"We'll be wonderful," Mabel purred.

"Promise me we'll have a full life," said Charles, "not all work."

Mabel agreed. They always planned to return to the Penny Bridge where they first courted, but by the time they did in late December of that year, it had been demolished and the Kosciuszko Bridge had been built in its place.

At the end of 1939, the year the World's Fair came to New York, and Burns battled with Allen on their Wednesday night radio show, Mabel and Charles were married on New Year's Eve at The Breakers Hotel in Palm Beach, registered under Mabel's new gentile name, Julianelli. For the first time she felt quite safe beyond the shtetl. On her feet Mabel wore a simple high heel – a black gabardine pump with a black patent leather bow, a style Charles designed for her, the same shoe he designed for Diana Vreeland many years later in a low-heel version.

By 1940 Mabel had two passions, her brand new husband and Schrafft's – specifically the vanilla sundae with a topping of hot butterscotch and whole salted almonds at Schrafft's.

Mabel lunched with her ladies at every possible opportunity. Charles' sisters, Annette and Jeanne, and his mother, Onorata, made the excursion from North Bergen to the East Seventy-Ninth Street Schrafft's lunchroom that Mabel liked the best. Sometimes joining her was Mabel's sister Helen, a nervous little woman, whose husband, Eli Davis, took away eventually to live in Miami.

From teenage years they were devoted to each
other but dared only to show their love many
years later. Honeymoon, 1940.

Dye-able satin, halter sandal, called the Honeymoon because Mabel wrapped the vamp with a thin gold-tone band, skyscraper heel: 3⅝ inches, 1960. Photograph by John Manno.

'Style with comfort'

The Julianellis set up shop, were established as Mabel Winkel & Co., and worked for commercial manufacturers who produced thousands of pairs of shoes a day from their designs. Before the Julianellis went into business, it was commonplace in the fashion business for pattern makers to design shoes. Initially, the Julianellis were hired to design patterns. But soon the Julianelli shoe designs became more important than the patterns, and manufacturers clamored for the whole shoe.

By 1941 they were the exclusive shoe designing team in the world. When other American shoe artists were selling sketches of their designs to manufacturers, the Julianellis were delivering leather pullovers. The manufacturers provided the lasts, wood molds of a foot in size 4B. The lasts lined the Julianellis' little sample factory, and varied from fragile and high-arched, built for high heels, to the corrective last, more solid and flatter, meant for low heels. Some were broader in the instep, some longer in the toe. The Julianellis drew their sample designs directly on the wood lasts.

Or a piece of fabric might be the inspiration for a design. Like a clothing designer drapes fabric on a form, Mabel draped, twisted and tacked the material to the wood last until it took shape as a workable shoe. She drew it on paper and Charles drew the pattern for the final shoe and perfected its construction. He cut and fitted little pieces of leather, satin and cloth together with the intricacy of a jigsaw puzzle. It was a highly technical job, familiar to him from his factory days and he worked with Vincent to cut the sample.

In 1940 Mabel and Charles applied for a United States Patent for a shoe construction which defied conventional construction. It was a *single-point attachment* of the vamp portion, and it attached the vamp to the sole and sock-lining by one or more lines of stitching, extending along the longitudinal center line of the shoe. 'The design enhances free lateral flexibility to the toe and enables that portion of the shoe to conform to irregularities in toe formation, and afford comfort in the toe portion of the shoe heretofore unknown,' noted the patent description from Mabel and Charles.

The Julianellis were soon synonymous with comfort. Besides, what was so great about Patent Number 2,234,066 by Mabel Winkel & Company was the whimsical triangular hole in the wedge heel. Mabel had an idea that a hole in the wedge would tickle Charles' fancy, and she set her mind to discovering for him other new titillations.

Opposite: The wood lasts, with which the Julianellis began a shoe concept (right to left): 1. With pencil sketch 2. Upper attached 3. With stripping, a heel, and knot tails, 1940-1970. Photograph by John Manno.

In 1940 their company name became Julianelli & Co., and working only under contract, they signed four design agreements immediately. The shoes sold from $6.50 to $22.50 a pair, with some selling for $90. One of their biggest manufacturers produced thirteen-thousand pairs a day, which sold all over the country and made them known for 'style with comfort at a low cost'. Another manufacturer made only five-hundred pairs a day, which was regarded in New York City as the decent number to produce – anything more was considered in poor taste. These shoes went to a New York store called Saks Fifth Avenue.

'The most talked of shoe of 1941—the Chopine', read the full-page Saks Fifth Avenue (Saks) ad in *The New York Times*, 'radical-startling-beautiful invention of the Julianellis, a sock and a sandal to wear separately or together. So simple and wonderful an idea that it was known—and then lost—four centuries ago. The Julianellis, adventurous, fantastically skillful, have recreated it for our times.

'You wear the sock for dinner at home,' the ad went on, 'the sandal alone or the complete Chopine (sock and sandal together) on white-tie evenings.'

Of the popularity of Julianelli's Chopine sandal there can be but one belief – it was a complete marvel, not for its balance, or its aerial support, or its spiraling single gold kid strap, but for the shrewdness of its shock value: the fact that a society woman would actually wear a *sock* to a white-tie event.

But they did, by the thousands! They wore the Chopine in its high heel construction or in Julianelli's patented Lift construction. *Vogue* gave it a full page as illustration of the coming season in its Fall Forecast editorial in the October 1, 1941 issue.

Of course Vincent had something to say as usual: "She wants us to make socks?" he whispered in Italian to Charles. "Basta cosi," replied Charles (meaning "enough already"), and Vincent never again opened his mouth about the Chopine or any of Mabel Julianelli's inventions. The Chopine was a delightful *fantasie* at a time when headlines spoke only of war.

With an increasing demand for Julianellis, the retail stores promoted them competitively, which was predictable after the debut of the Chopine. A year later, in 1942, the Metropolitan Museum of Art was the recipient of a Saks Fifth Avenue gift of two pairs of Julianelli shoes, given as a donation to their Costume Institute: a medium heel pump with a top-stitched bow in brown leather, and one of the Julianellis' popular satin dancing sandals in navy. These shoes became part of the Costume Institute's permanent collection until they were gifted by the museum to Parsons The New School For Design.

"My mother, Annette Leyden and Aunt Mabel had so much fun together. I used to laugh at their relationship. I brought Mom to Aunt Mabel's apartment in New York from Albany, where we lived, on the bus and we took a taxi cab from Port Authority to East Eighty-Sixth Street. When they were together, it was like watching two older people kidding around and it was foreign to me being in my early twenties. It made me laugh. I got a real chuckle out of it. They were wonderful people, the two of them."

John Charles Leyden
Mabel's nephew

Opposite: Sister-in-law Annette and Mabel model the first shoes designed for Saks Fifth Avenue, 1940.

SAKS FIFTH AVE NEWS

dancing shoes to glitter through the season's festivities

from a gem-like collection in the shoe salon, fourth floor.

Left: Saks Fifth Avenue dancing shoes, 1942. Saks Fifth Avenue.
Opposite: 'Stocking-Fit-Pump', 1942. Saks Fifth Avenue.

The Julianelli Chopine sandal at the Museum of Modern Art. Installation view of the exhibition,
'Are Clothes Modern?' at the Museum of Modern Art, New York (November 28, 1944-March 4,
1945). Two Julianelli Chopine Sandals are photographed top left, lent by Saks Fifth Avenue.
Digital Image © The Museum of Modern Art/Licensed by SCALA/Art Resource, NY.

Two years later the Museum of Modern Art included two Julianelli Chopines loaned by Saks, in an exhibition entitled 'Are Clothes Modern?' from November 28th through March 4th, 1945. The Saks November 8th invoice read: 'Pair shoes, red suede sandals, designed Julianelli, Pair shoes, black suede, designed Julianelli, Pair shoes, red suede sock, designed Julianelli.'

Mabel had contracts, but she did not have *carte blanche*. This was one of the essentials she was missing. She would work with store buyers, but she was a leader, and she told Charles to tell them so.

What siphoned Julianelli confidence into the major department and specialty stores, starting in New York City and spreading out across the nation from there, was Mabel's instinct when it came to the simplest shoe. The stores showed a certain timidity concerning simplicity, but Mabel proved to Saks Fifth Avenue that an undemanding and effortless carriage for a woman's foot was best. For example, their suede pump with a treatment on the vamp and a sliver-thin platform for cushion – the Stocking-Fit-Pump – became history-making for Saks, who sold seventy-five-thousand pairs by August of 1942.

Saks offered to get behind the Julianellis as couturiers one hundred percent, and give them that missing carte blanche.

However, they would not allow the trademark name, Julianelli, to go on the insole, and the shoes were sold under the Saks Fifth Avenue label.

Creative moment: Mabel in her Brooklyn studio, 1940.

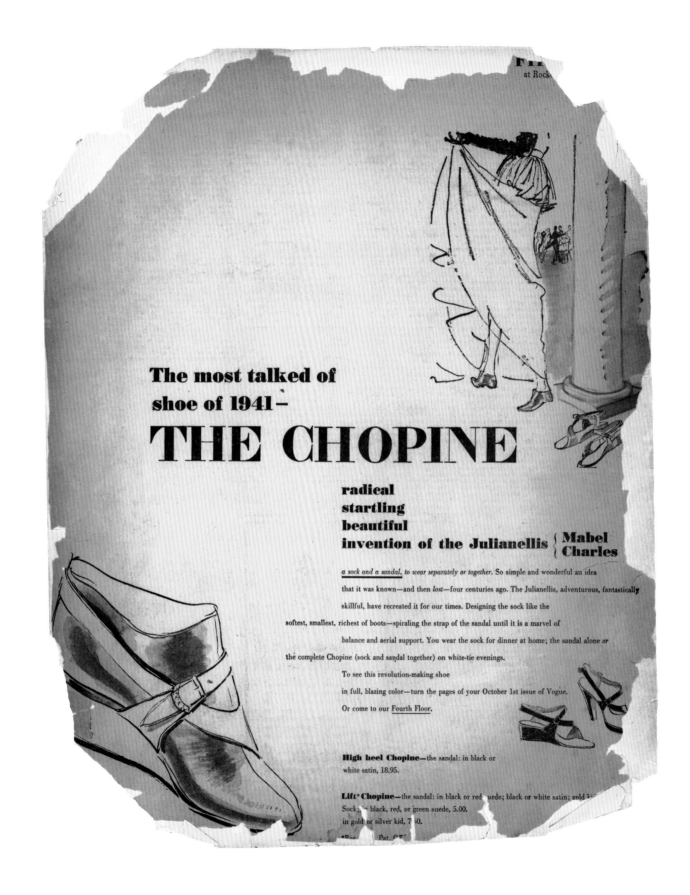

The most talked of
shoe of 1941—

THE CHOPINE

radical
startling
beautiful
invention of the Julianellis { **Mabel** **Charles**

a sock and a sandal, to wear separately or together. So simple and wonderful an idea

that it was known—and then *lost*—four centuries ago. The Julianellis, adventurous, fantastically

skillful, have recreated it for our times. Designing the sock like the

softest, smallest, richest of boots—spiraling the strap of the sandal until it is a marvel of

balance and aerial support. You wear the sock for dinner at home; the sandal alone *or*

the complete Chopine (sock and sandal together) on white-tie evenings.

To see this revolution-making shoe

in full, blazing color—turn the pages of your October 1st issue of Vogue.

Or come to our Fourth Floor.

High heel Chopine—the sandal: in black or
white satin, 18.95.

Lift· Chopine—the sandal: in black or red suede; black or white satin; gold k
Sock: black, red, or green suede, 5.00.
in gold or silver kid, 7 50.

·Reg Pat OT·

OPPOSITE—Newest shoe is the chopine, designed by Mabel and Charles Julianelli. Naked satin sandal plus gold kid sock. Wear each separately, too. Taffeta dress. All; Saks-Fifth Avenue. (More on page 111)

Opposite: Saks Fifth Avenue ad for the Chopine sandal, 1941. Saks Fifth Avenue.
Top right: Chopine sandal in *Vogue*, 1941, introducing Fall Forecast Editorial Page in caption. John Rawlings/Condé Nast Archive; Copyright © Condé Nast Publications.
Bottom right: Chopine sandal, photo caption from *Vogue*, 1941. John Rawlings/Condé Nast Archive; Copyright © Condé Nast Publications.

March 9, 1959

The Julianellis flew over the Aegean Sea on Pan American,
Flight 8, from Istanbul, Turkey, to New Delhi, India,
with stops in Ankara and Teheran. Mabel made Charles do the
talking, and was as happy as she could be, but his drive and
ambition seemed spent after thirty years designing shoes.
Mabel knew he was anxiously thinking: 'Once again we are
traveling,' while she was gleefully thinking, 'Oh, the price
of fame!'

Flying over the Aegean, in those moments when they were
not within miles of any country, Mabel's thoughts turned back
to the year before, when they were flying on Capital Airlines'
luxury Viscount Flight 77 to Alabama, to be presented to the
press as V.I.Ps, and bestow the Best-Dressed List of 1958
during Birmingham's Fall Fashion Week, adopted from Eleanor
Lambert's International Best-Dressed List.

The Birmingham Post-Herald devoted half a page to
a picture of a smiling, waving group of people, including
the Julianellis, descending the plane. The group was
euphemistically called star-studded however lacking in
other designers — there were a couple of national retail
merchandise managers, sales managers, and a representative
of a ready-to-wear firm. That was usually the composition
of these types of public appearances.

On the bottom half of the page was a Blach's ad, showing
the Day and Night shoe, 'the shoe with the button that
turns dark for day and bright by night', announcing that
the Julianellis would be in the ladies' shoe salon all day
to demonstrate their tricky shoe.

Of course this button ornament had scandalized Vincent,
back in the New York sample room, but he said nothing, as much
as he wanted to. There was a lot of eye-rolling and Vincent
did that until the day he retired from Julianelli Inc.

After the ceremony Mabel found Charles in the bar of Birmingham's Dinkler-Tutwiler Hotel with one of the Best Dressed having cocktails, hard put to say anything that made sense, the prominent socialite, sitting beside him, eyeing Mabel the way women do when they feel sorry for the wife.

"Darlin', is that your wife?" Mabel heard Best Dressed blurt out to Charles, "Damn, she's not good lookin' enough for you."

Mabel's sister Helen had warned her before she married Charles, "You know Charles, when he gets in the mood of the bumble bee he has to get it out of his system..." That was true, thought Mabel, but only when it came to his portrait painting. He would leave town and not return until the portrait recipient had a likeness of himself in his hands. But, to Mabel's knowledge, it had never been true about women.

"He will most likely come back and be so happy with you," Helen said. Helen Davis, a petite, cigarette-smoking bundle of nerves, was unhappy in her marriage. "Mabel dear," Helen said, "he might be having a change of life. Men go through that the same as women."

A certain sweet quality in Charles' manner prevented Mabel from concluding any infidelity. However, because of her sister's concern, whether or not Helen indulged in observations on her own marriage, Mabel let the thought cross over her mind as surely but swiftly as a slight headache.

She continued to think of her husband as an adorable adolescent who hadn't wised up yet. Charles let women get the best of him without meaning to. That Southern Belle had probably found him sitting alone in the cocktail lounge, and had plopped on him like a perfumed pile of mud.

On the plane, his Adonis good looks showed splendidly in the eerie light of the sky above the clouds, and looking over at him, Mabel could see how his hair had evenly grayed, pepper and salt. He was leaner now. She always knew when he was thinking of his younger days painting — his eyes darkened under furrowed brows.

The move to Manhattan

Mabel and Charles soon moved their operation to Manhattan and incorporated. The letterhead on the new stationery read: 'Julianelli Inc., 47 West 34th Street, New York 1, N.Y.'

The new offices were in the Marbridge Building across from R.H. Macy & Co., in Herald Square, that piece of land which began as fields, bushes and unnamed roads, then dancehalls and bordellos, and then a square named Greeley. The history alone appealed to the Julianellis, with everything that was exciting about New York converging in their direction: Macy's and its neighborhood, in which other ladies' fashion emporiums in the era of the Big Store were built, such as B. Altman & Co. on Madison Avenue and Thirty-Fourth Street.

For Mabel, Macy's was a wonderful place of memories, the place where she and Charles had set the date for their marriage. Later, Altman's would be special too; it would be the place where she would take her young daughter to lunch in the Charleston Gardens.

Mabel Julianelli was a charming woman, but charm took a maddening amount of patience. It took every iota of charm she possessed not to become unglued at the thought – day after day – of shoe after shoe going to leading manufacturers, without the trademark Julianelli on the insole.

Nearly twenty other patents for Julianelli shoe constructions, designs for a shoe, designs for a decorative piece for footwear, even a glove construction, were applied for in the next two years.

Other shoe companies some sixty years later would consult these patents for their lasting relevancy, among them Jimmy Choo Ltd. in Great Britain, Nike Inc., Bata-Schuh AG in Switzerland, Global Brand Marketing Inc., France's Salomon S.A., and Siebe Gorman & Co., Ltd, Great Britain, for the glove construction.

Charles patented a new construction in which he shaped the upper directly into its final shape and desired size. He stated in the application, dated November 24th, 1942, 'It is among the objects of my invention to produce a shoe or slipper that will 'fit like a glove', having definite utility as well as a pleasing design and appearance.'

Mabel had *carte blanche* but she did not have brand identity. This was the last essential missing. Saks would promote their work, but the shoes were advertised 'By Saks Fifth Avenue', without the

Julianelli name. Some ads that carried Julianelli shoes were really promoting Saks' Elvette cloth glove fabric or their Fenton last, with the Julianelli brand very much in the background. Mabel would not be in the background for long.

The Julianellis' first rented Manhattan apartment was at 20 Fifth Avenue. In 1942 they moved to their second apartment, 33 East End Avenue. It had a little terrace overlooking the East River, and it was here that the most important events of their lives would occur. Mabel and Charles spent a lot of time on that terrace talking about their life together so far.

One romantic evening, when the moon clipped the top corner of a gaudy neon billboard somewhere behind Ward's Island, they sat together on an iron bench as Mabel called to mind her eighteenth birthday party, when she had tricked a boy named Carl into announcing their engagement.

"I never in my life was more surprised," Charles said, snuggling closer to her.

"I probably wished that Carl had not picked that occasion for the surprise," Mabel said girlishly.

"You mean you didn't get that poor kid to propose to you just to rope me in?" said Charles, "Sure you did."

"Sure I did," Mabel said. "Maybe I shouldn't have married you at all. Everyone's been against it."

"Not everyone," said Charles, "not Mama."

It was true about his Mama. Charles' mother had accepted their marriage.

Veiled behind her Italian last name in business relations, Mabel would hear anti-Semitic slurs among her peers and the words would stay with her. To make matters worse, her family disapproved of the marriage and she was bereft of those relatives for a lifetime, including her mother, Essie. The exceptions were Essie's two sisters, Minnie Friedman and Bertha Robinson. Bertha, a romantic, fell in love with the fine person Charles was, and included them in Jewish holiday dinners. Minnie lived down the block from Bertha and was accordingly influenced. It was no coincidence that later as adults, Minnie's son Steve and Bertha's daughter Anne would be close cousins of Mabel's, even though as children they lived in Crown Heights and did not visit Mabel often.

Onorata would not tolerate anything being said against her daughter-in-law. Charles' girlfriends, violins, cars, portraits, indecision, instability, and caprice had all disappeared with Mabel's devotion and guidance. She loved Mabel and Mabel loved her back. The Julianellis became Mabel's family.

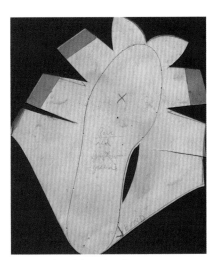

Charles Julianelli for Julianelli Inc.
Pattern for patented ready-cut shoe
upper construction, 1942.

Very Saks Fifth Avenue:

Hand Carved Leathers

**exciting variations
by our famous
young shoe designers,
Mabel and Charles Julianelli.**

**Shoe Salon,
Fourth Floor**

Platforms and
buckles with strange prehistoric
plants and animals **carved**
painstakingly out of leather . . . like some
stone age cave drawing.
In soft, supple leathers
. . . polished to saddle sheen.

**Shoe Salon,
Fourth Floor**

Red, brown, tan, beige or blue calf with hand **carved**
platform and trim. **18.95** Tan,
beige or blue calf with hand **carved**
platform and trim. **18.95**

Hand carved bag
18.75.
Hand carved belt
5.00.
Street Floor Accessories

'Very Saks Fifth Avenue: Hand Carved Leathers',
1942. Saks Fifth Avenue.

Shoestring bow cut-out spectator pump,
toe-tip, heel, collar, trim and bow in snakeskin,
rest of upper in suede, heel 2¼ inches, 1950.
Photograph by John Manno.

The soft-as-butter color, stiletto heel and
pointed toe made this shoe a spring sensation
from Dallas to Schenectady, double band at
collar ending in toe knot, heel, 3¾ inches, 1958.
Photograph by John Manno.

Pearl open-shank day slipper, heel, 2⅝ inches, 1980. Courtesy of Iris Friedman. Photograph by John Manno.

Julianelli in the news

During the 1940s, Mabel sketched, prying her talent open until everything came pouring out. Every shoe invention one has ever heard of – and thought was new or modern – originally came from Mabel Julianelli. Syndicated columnist Alice Hughes rattled off Team Julianelli's accomplishments in her 'New York Report' column in a 1947 issue of the *New York Herald:*

From the record come these 'firsts' credited to this married shoe team; they were first with cork clog. They originated the first one-piece shoe ever made in modern times. The ballet street shoe is their idea. The Chopine, a sandal with a thong worn over a suede sock, an ancient footwear inspiration is made wearable in the present by Charles and Mabel. Also the laced-in-back shoe, the high-back shoe, the revised T-strap, and two-strap anklet, the scalloped shoe silhouette, a million new shoe constructions to make it pleasant to walk, and the newest dancing slipper—an Irene Castle inspiration with back, heel and straps of satin matching the color of an evening dress, while the front is a neutral shade. This record could go on, but the point is that the Julianellis are in the lead in creative shoe ideas that find wide approval and sales.

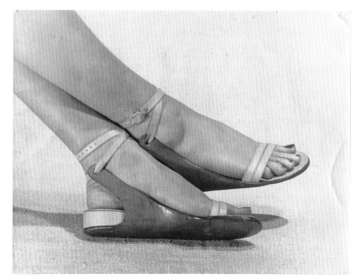

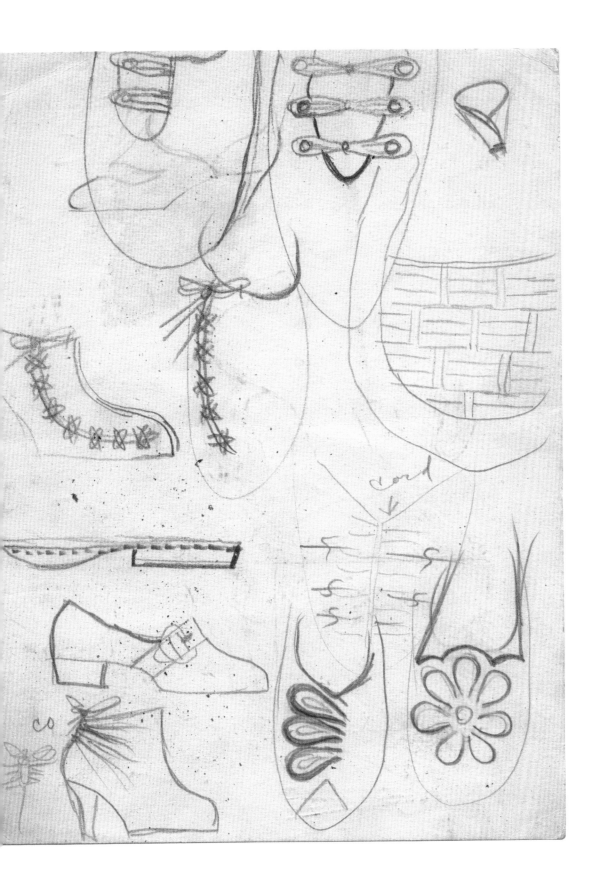

Opposite bottom left: The Irene Castle shoe, 1941.
Opposite bottom centre: Mabel Julianelli for Julianelli Inc. Sketch of laced-in-back shoe, 1948. © 2010 Jane Julianelli.
Opposite bottom right: One piece shoe, 1943
This page: Mabel Julianelli for Mabel Winkel & Co. Sketches including, her monk-strap (fourth row), laced-in-back shoe (bottom left), cutouts (bottom), 1941. © 2010 Jane Julianelli.

christmas special!

B
for Big
evenings:
sophia, long on luxury!

Sophia Loren wearing evening sandals derived
from the signature naked sandal by Mabel
Julianelli, 1982. As seen in US *Harper's Bazaar*.

For holiday nights, Sophia Loren celebrates with the season's most exuberantly ruffled and beaded dresses in opulent fabrics shaped to show off her figure—or yours!

She is one of the few actresses who is—and almost always has been—recognized as much for her talent as for her extraordinary beauty. "Sometimes, when you're too pretty, people see you and don't hear you," says Sophia who, once she got her career off the ground, carefully chose the most difficult and complicated roles she could find to avoid being typecast.

"When I was young, my aim was to be a serious actress—not a sex symbol whose starring time was limited by her youthful beauty." This was all for the most practical reasons: "I had to support myself and my family.

(CONTINUED ON PAGE 208)

A generously draped, long-sleeved long dress in off-white with gray bugle beads at the neck, opposite page, inset: By John Anthony, about $1,150. At Saks Fifth Avenue; D. H. Holmes, New Orleans; Esther Wolf, Houston; Amen Wardy, Newport Beach, CA. Earrings by Paloma Picasso for Tiffany & Co. Extravagantly ruffled and every bit as beautiful as Sophia, left: An off-the-shoulder, bias-cut red silk dress with organza ruffles around the neck and cuff. By Stavropoulos, about $2,450. At Martha, NYC, Palm Beach, Bal Harbour; John Wanamaker; D. H. Holmes, New Orleans; Neiman-Marcus; Neusteters, Denver. Earrings from Cartier. Sandals, Julianelli. For a body as great-looking as Sophia's, try her new Sophia Body Spa Collection from Coty. Hair by Harry King.

The stores and their customers swept Mabel and Charles high enough to catch the interest of the press, and the press in turn flew them up to the fashion authorities who sat, somewhat sprung in the seat from all the criticizing they had to do.

Saks Fifth Avenue was the first store to acknowledge the Julianelli artistry in the early 1940s. They promoted them in a big way, and it was Saks who understood the vision of the Julianellis – they were doing something which had not been done before in shoe design and construction, and Saks understood the inventiveness of their new *single point attachment* construction. Saks was followed by Volk in Dallas, Bullock's Wilshire in Los Angeles, Lord & Taylor and Bonwit Teller in New York, and Burdine's in Miami.

The only enthusiasts more devoted than the stores were the newspapers: 'The Julianellis are as young and attractive as the shoes they design,' wrote reporter Grace Davidson for the *New York Post*. 'This is immediately apparent. Today the Julianellis are the only exclusive shoe-designing team in the field.' The first young designing married couple in shoe fashion sparked interest and sentiment, and besides, they were so cute. As early as 1941, their reputation was circulating: a young, American married couple, dominating the all-male Italian fashion domain of shoe design. The Julianellis' story was told in a variety of papers, from the big city *The New York Times*, to the homespun *Kingsport Times* in Tennessee, which reported: 'It is the story of two young people, each with a fervor for drawing and painting, who started their separate paths in art school.'

Newspapers featured the introverted Mabel and the outgoing Charles:

> 'Designing shoes is my method of art expression,' Mabel was quoted in the Herald of Grand Rapids, Michigan. 'I may have a deep feeling for a certain type of architecture, and in some way I convert it into the lines of a shoe,' she said for the Free Press of Mankato, Minnesota.

'Mabel and Charles Julianelli predict high-button shoes, and the chances are you'll be wearing 'em,' wrote California's *Oakland Tribune*. 'Each season they design trend shoes for a number of the country's largest shoe manufacturers. They estimate that 50,000 pairs of shoes a day are made from their designs.'

They were written up in *Collier's* after Mabel dyed her hair a hard-hitting peroxide blond, which gave her the appearance of a young Bette Davis or a young Shirley Temple in drag, and made her the sensation of the Barberry Room. Reporters loved the hair, but went in more for the topic of Mabel

The Julianelli Two-Strap Anklet
from Sketch to Shoe
Mabel Winkel for Mabel Winkel & Co. Sketches
including 1941 two-strap anklet, second row.
© 2010 Jane Julianelli.

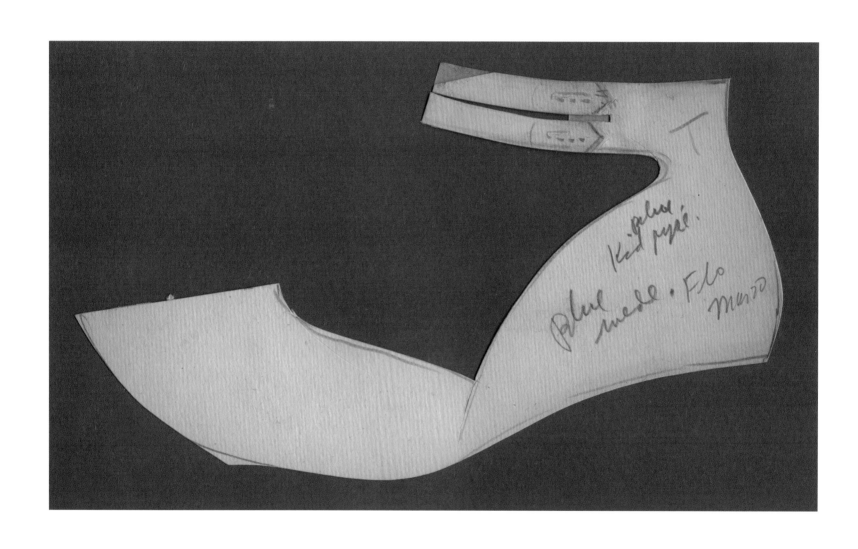

Opposite: Two-strap anklet, 1942.
Above: Charles Julianelli for Mabel Winkel & Co.
Pattern of two-strap anklet, blue suede buckled, 1941.

April 1947

and Charles' mutual admiration – Mabel said, 'Charles thinks up our most original, unexpected ideas; but I get most of the credit,' and Charles said, 'Mabel sees right away how to adapt and work out an idea to make a good shoe.' They were the Alphonse and Gaston of the shoe business, according to the *Collier's* reporter.

All of Mabel's designs in every shoe shape, style, and fabrication, from the sophisticated to the playful, were coming from her pencil to paper faster than Charles and Vincent could make the samples. Manufacturers and fashion pundits didn't know how to handle her, or what to call her inspirations. It is suggested that columnist Alice Hughes coined the phrase 'fashion firsts', and it stuck. Now Mabel secured their brand name on the insole: her sweeping signature – Julianelli – stamped in gold.

In the early part of the 1940s, Mabel's goal was to make American women more comfortable with their patriotism, less lonely without their men, perhaps as a guarantee against a threatening war. One design was a closed toe, low heeled pump which looked right with the new wartime cotton stockings. A pairing was born and it was all the rave – the Julianelli shoe and the cotton stocking.

"We women don't need silk and nylon," she told *The Philadelphia Inquirer*, when the war brought on a shortage. She was in part reacting to the press, which was making American women feel deprived without them. "There's much to love about the new cotton stockings in wine, moss green, bright red, purple and white mesh." It was the first time that Mabel had spoken to the press without Charles. She became heroic when she was strong in her conviction.

In a New York daily, reporter Dana Jenney wrote: 'Highlighted in the Saks Fifth Avenue shoe collection were a number of designs by Mabel and Charles Julianelli who have introduced many startlingly new fashions in shoes. Beginning the show was a group of sports, country and walking shoes, and believe us they were a far cry from the brogans that used to be serviceable and nothing else, except that they usually wore like iron, and felt like iron ... the Julianelli design touch in the low heeled dress shoe, an invention for the woman who is allergic to high heels, was a hand crocheted wool edging around the buckle ... one pair of black crepe evening slippers boasted 1,800 studded colored stones.'

Opposite: Insoles with Mabel Julianelli's signature. This group ranges between 1940-1970. Photograph by John Manno.

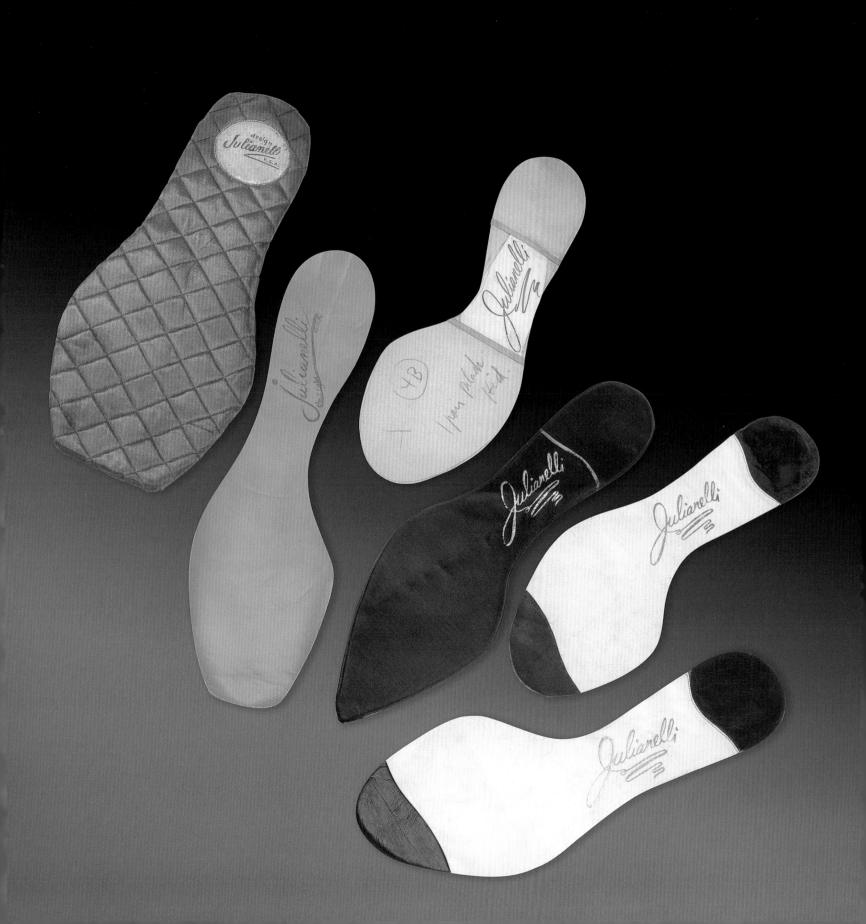

Stepping out

The business of the Julianellis was not always to make glamorous shoes, but to make the simple ones intriguing. It took reflection and a great deal of spaghetti. Both were given in good supply on Sundays at Onorata and Luigi's home, a two-story brick house at 30 Eighth Street in Fairview, New Jersey, the house Mabel and Charles bought for his parents, and their only suburban destination out of New York City. They had rented an apartment for Papa Winkel in Brooklyn, but did not visit.

The house and garden in Fairview were very Italian and very Catholic. There was a painted Madonna over the couch and Onorata's crochet doily on the couch. There were plum tomatoes and tiny cherry tomatoes planted in the garden behind the house and a figurine of St Anthony in front of the house.

They were a group of nine: Mama and Pop, Jeanne and Joe, Annette and Jack, Mabel and Charles, and Papa Winkel sometimes joined in. In the garden where everyone took in some sun, Mabel drew sketches mentally; while making the rounds of the tomatoes, she noted two stems lying across each other, with clusters of infant tomatoes hanging off each end. Such a luxurious arrangement in nature could be a buckle on a shoe.

Every time she saw rhinestones, she thought of tomatoes. She tried an overlay of rhinestones. That shoe she named the Mae West.

It was the extent of their socializing, the little family of nine, until one day, with added self-assurance due to her platinum hair, Mabel resolved that they must go clubbing in New York.

In 1942 dim joints with foreign names, exotic drinks and flashing-eyed dancers abounded in and around Fiftieth Street and Broadway: La Conga, Café Zanzibar, Havana Madrid, Club Samoa, and the Hawaiian Room, not to be confused with Hawaii Kai or Luau 400. Then there were the Rooms, smarter and further uptown: the Persian Room of the Plaza Hotel, the Maisonette Room of the St Regis, the Barberry Room of the Berkshire, and the Empire Room of the Waldorf Astoria. Mabel, who loved Charles James, but felt rather too short for his lavish ball gowns, mainly wore tailored Norman Norell of Traina-Norell. Norell, also a Pratt Institute student and her mentor, taught her that one superior dress was worth a closet full of inferior ones.

Mabel Revised the T-Strap
This page: Little-T, 1948.
Opposite: The Little T t-strap revisited, designed for the Empire look in the '40s and then revised in the '60s, mid-heel: 2½ inches. Photograph by John Manno.

Again Alice Hughes was on their trail, carousing with Mabel and Charles in the Barberry Room. 'To look at her you'd never believe she probably creates more shoe styles for women than any other person in the country...' Hughes reported in her column, 'A Woman's New York' for the Hearst Syndicate, '...she's a mite of a thing, with big dark eyes and a mountainous blond pompadour. Her clothes are simple and good, and you can bet her shoes are the latest word. She always wears high spike heels.'

When shortages of goods dominated the headlines and leather supplies were severely curtailed, as were fabrics, manufacturers and stores screamed for innovative alternatives. The shoe business, really the whole fashion business, was desperate to keep working. The war had sapped everything and the shortages were noticeable. For Mabel, resourceful as ever, there was a hospitable audience waiting for her new suede or imitation reptile on calf. She spoke frequently to the press over the phone, though Charles handled the face-to-face interviews.

That year she told *The Christian Science Monitor*, 'Calfskin will be the important shoe of the year—and the patriotic one. Blacks and browns will predominate. There will be many tans done much in the feeling of the Army tradition. Women are going to appreciate the need for lower heels.

Who needs to run around town collecting for the Armed Forces in stilettos?

We feel this is the time to keep shoes comfortable, fitting and ladylike. Shoes, like clothes, express the spirit of the times.'

Against the backdrop of war in Europe, New York City rebelled with a high dose of civility. Against the backdrop of prejudice in her own family Mabel rebelled with a high dose of aspirin. One must understand the nature of Mabel and Charles' *mixed* marriage – it mixed everybody up. Mabel was taught by her political father about the strain between Jews and Italian Americans, how troubled the two communities were to begin with, with rivalry for jobs in the garment industry, for immigrant housing, for union representation, made all the worse by Mussolini's Fascism in Europe.

Mabel shunned politics and she shunned prejudice, almost as if they were one and the same. The opportunity that her childhood had given her for despising both had resulted in her resolve to never indulge in either. She carried under her blond pompadour an inventory of every creative and talented person in New York, regardless of their race, color or interests and was happiest when any number of these people joined her in doing something creative.

Mabel Revised the T-Strap
Opposite: Mabel Julianelli for Julianelli Inc. Sketches of pumps and the earliest versions of the Little-T t-strap, 1946. © 2010 Jane Julianelli. *Opposite right:* Charles Julianelli for Julianelli Inc. Pattern of toeless, black suede, gold cutout t-strap, 1943.

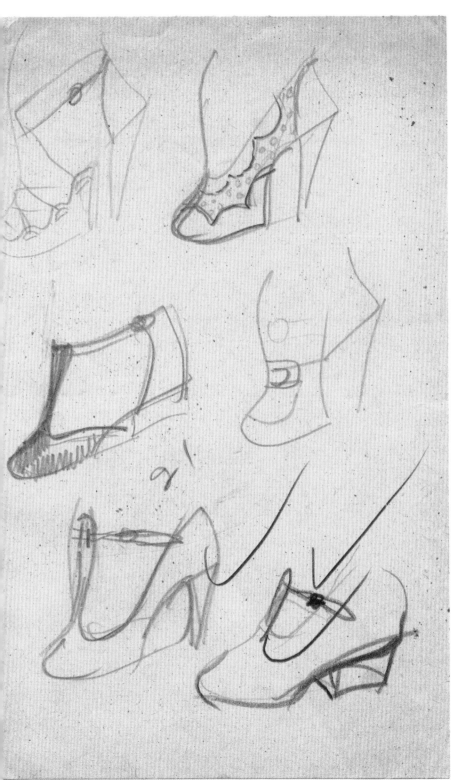

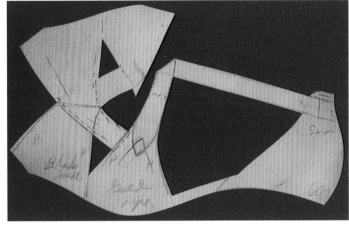

Perhaps Papa Winkel had poisoned the family against her for marrying Charles. Perhaps it was her mother. The circumstances around the suicide of Elena, Charles' former girlfriend, did not tell her much, just that she felt it was her first close brush with bigotry and not her last.

Charles started smoking at this time, perhaps conceding to the popular affect of the Don Juans in the Persian Room, or excusing the habit with the notion that he and Mabel were, in all aspects, rebels, or because of worry. Often Mabel found that he had disappeared into the hallway in front of their offices in Room 850 of the Marbridge Building, and was leaning against a metal pipe, smoking and staring at the mosaic tile floor.

Mabel, in contrast to him, was strong despite what was going on around her. As long as her mind remained unruffled by the war, because Charles was with her and not in it, she continued to be a Jewish Pollyanna.

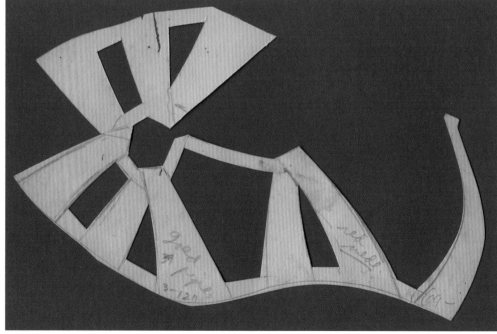

Reptile

Reptile

Mabel Revised the T-Strap
Opposite: Band of Charm t-strap, 1943.
Opposite: Charles Julianelli for Julianelli Inc.
Pattern of red suede with gold piping
evening t-strap sandal, 1942.
Left: Mabel Julianelli for Julianelli Inc. sketches
in reptiles, 1942. © 2010 Jane Julianelli.

"The heck with shortages"

In 1942 Charles enlisted in the National Guard. Charles called from work to tell her. Mabel, who had been busy moving their belongings in a Crescent Cab, from their old apartment at 20 Fifth Avenue to their new apartment at 33 East End Avenue, dropped her packages on Ninth Street, and fainted into the arms of a doorman. On December 1st, 1943, Charles was called to join Company A as a private, along with sixteen-hundred other men, during the Army's mobilization. They were stationed at Camp Upton in Yaphank, Long Island.

"Turn the clock back to yesterday," Mabel cried, even though he'd only be sixty miles away. Charles came into their apartment the night after his news, smoking one of his Camels unfiltered, in a tweed winter coat, a garment bag over one arm, a bottle of Soave Bolla under the other, and walked to the living room picture window, unzipping the garment bag to reveal an army uniform. He told Mabel he would be reporting to base later that week.

Charles led Mabel onto the terrace, settling them down on the bench to talk about their life together while looking at the river, throwing his coat over her. She stretched out her little feet in her Band of Charm T-straps until her toes could touch the balcony, bawling, "Must you go?" She always wore her sexiest styles in private with Charles.

Mabel, heartsick to see Charles off at the Penn Station platform, was squeezed tightly into a herd of weeping women, all hats and Joan Crawford shoulders.

"Nonsense," she argued with herself, sizing up the situation, working her big brown eyes up and down the disappearing caboose, the divine smell of his cigarette smoke floating on her lips. "Of course he'll be back, the same as always."

'Last night,' Mabel wrote in her first letter to him, 'I slept alone for the first time – I don't like to be alone – but, then, the only one I really care to sleep with is you. I do like to think about you, darling – even though your letters could be more lovey-dovey – but I know you will do better as time goes by. I remember that Mama told me that when your Pop went to the Wars she didn't hear from him for two years. You can't do that to me! Sometimes in bed I turn over to your side and hang on to your pillow a little – and

Gee, honey I know that I will become a camp follower like all the other dames…'

Mabel Chose the Right Heel with the Right Toe

Opposite inset: Charles Julianelli for Julianelli Inc. Pattern for pump with circle rhinestone ornament and large grosgrain bow, made exclusively for Diana Vreeland; grosgrain swatch and circle attached, 1960.
Opposite: Diana Vreeland's pump, the tailored evening shoe, made exclusively for her by Charles, with a low heel because of her height, a rhinestone circle ornament, squared toe, oversized bow, heel: 1¾ inches, mid 1960s. Photograph by John Manno.
Next spread left: Eugenia Sheppard called this shoe 'brilliant'. Stiletto dress pump for Mabel's black tie events, heel: 3¾ inches, 1950. Photograph by John Manno.
Next spread right: The Strip-tease jeweled evening mule, satin/rhinestone stripping, heel: 3½ inches, late 1960. Courtesy of Iris Friedman. Photograph by John Manno.

It was 2 am one morning when Mabel sat alone in her new bedroom facing the East River, lit by the glorious neon letters of the billboard. She could never make out what the words said, but the eyesore was possibly what she liked best about the view. Charles chose the apartment building because he could park his 1943 Chrysler in the cul-de-sac by the John Finley boardwalk of Carl Schultz Park.

Mabel wondered how her body could produce so many sobs. What if he died? What had she done to Charles? She pushed him in a direction in which he never wanted to be pushed. She should have pursued her dream of being an architect and let him pursue his of being a portrait painter. It could have worked. She thought only for a minute, the time it took her breath to rise and fall. She could see them in a little Brooklyn flat, Charles painting portraits if commissions ever came along, and Mabel cleaning buildings rather than designing them.

She was not irreverent about Charles' dream, a dream that had gotten him a mention once in *Time* magazine from 1928. The article on President Coolidge noted that one Charles A. Julianelli, a shoe-factory worker, aged 20, of Union City, had called at the White House to give President Coolidge a portrait for which Charles had used three photographs for models. When interviewed, Charles told how he had had to wait while some Congressmen were talking with the President, how the secretary, Mr Sanders, brought him in, and how he was nervous at first, but began to feel better after shaking hands. He went on to say that he told the President he hoped he wouldn't consider it flattering, not wanting the portrait to appear better than the man himself. The President said it was a good likeness and Charles stayed for twenty minutes.

That was Charles' dream but now Mabel had to face reality. She went back to a grueling routine, the only cure-all she could think of. She was running the business alone. The first thing she wanted to convey was comfort, comfort, comfort: 'Women have gone beyond the era of heavy corseting, either of their bodies or their feet. Shoes should be soft, pliable and glove-like,' she said. She remembered the clunkers her mother wore, which broke Essie's feet before Essie could break them in.

More artisans were hired, Leo and Eddie who were Italian, and Sam who was a Russian Jew – all singers who crooned in Italian or Yiddish, or an occasional barber-shop quartet rendition of broken English. When she hired a feisty 4B foot model Phyllis Teschon, a platinum blond, Mabel dyed her hair back to her natural brown. She wasn't about to compete every day in an imitation Jean Harlow contest.

Charles' youngest sister, Jeanne was hired as Mabel's secretary, and Betty Noonan as her assistant. Neither woman had any practical office experience. Both were always on the verge of a nervous

Above: Proud of his Italian roots, he was most proud to be an American. Charles, the Army man, in World War II, 1944.
Opposite: The day before he left for Fort Warren, Wyoming, Mabel and Charles visited his parents in Fairview, New Jeresey and posed with his sister, Jeanne, 1944.

breakdown over their men in the Armed Forces. They were excitable and girlish. They were frenzied, frantic, almost rabid. Betty wailed over each letter her husband Bert sent from North Africa. Jeanne was desperate to be near Joe, about to ship out from Marshfield, California. Mabel tried to instruct Jeanne and take the Boop out of Betty, but with little luck. She wouldn't think of firing them. It made her look forward to dinner with Cousin Anne Robinson, who didn't have a husband. Mabel learned that American women everywhere were terrified for their men, and could not hide it, even in the workplace, and that stuck with her.

Mabel had seen her husband go to war. She had buried her mother. She had been a dutiful daughter to her father. In 1943 she thought it was high time she bought a new wardrobe. She had to get glamorous, prettier and thinner for her visits to see Charles on base.

A month after Charles left, she wrote to him that she had been shopping at Saks Fifth Avenue with Cousin Anne for slender suit blazers, more contoured to her body, blouses, skirts, and a cute little number whipped up by Hattie Carnegie that sat magnificently on her head, asking nothing of her average brown hair. There was less fabric to make anything, consequently her blouses were thin viscose, and her skirts were pleat-less. She felt insecure about becoming a stunner in slim skirts and see-through blouses, but if she must, she must.

Mabel needed materials. Because it was wartime, no decorative trim or elaborate stitching was allowed on shoes, no extra buttons – three the limit – and very few materials, no lacing, no metals, no rhinestones, no beads.

'Can't you send me back anything from Yaphank?' she begged Charles in her letters.

Mabel's letters were either lovey-dovey, or they complained over and over about the lack of materials to make shoe ornaments. Once Mr Gimbel said hello and gave her a big handshake, impressing Cousin Anne. Saks Fifth Avenue at that time was a subsidiary of Gimbel Brothers, Inc. Mabel was buying a cashmere scarf for Charles.

'"Keep up the good work", Mr Gimbel told me,' wrote Mabel, 'but how can I when I have to resort to cucumber slices?'

Mabel got a letter from Charles right away because she called him crying every night at 9 pm. He sent her a locket. As he had the foresight to join the National Guard Charles was soon promoted to an acting sergeant. Knowing he was in a safer position, Mabel still suffered in his absence.

He wrote in passing that he had made friends on base. Leaving aside the question of Mabel's misgivings at the thought of her big, handsome man out in the world without her, she collected herself calmly and wrote, 'I am very happy that you met some nice men and had lunch with them. Somehow, I think this was something very important in your life that you missed and I hope you will continue some of the fine acquaintances after the war is over.'

By the end of 1943 Charles was sketching shoes – in his spare time, in his sleep – from whichever army base he was sent to – New York, Virginia, Wyoming.

He was that kind of man, wanting to do the best for his wife and the best for his country all at the same time.

'Have just received the camouflaged design,' wrote Mabel, who insisted to herself and everyone around her that the war would soon be over. It had to be. 'I think the one with the three tones, lighter on the bottom, is a stunning idea, however, I would not tie this up with camouflage as I believe women will not want anything associated with the war in the post-war era.' By now she was designing for other shoe companies like Palter De Liso. The next letter would read: 'Gee honey, the sunsets over the river have been so beautiful – I just love them – I try to imagine you are here too. It doesn't work.'

Even towards the end of the war the future looked very bleak. 'I can hardly believe that I ever saw a woman smiling,' wrote Mabel. Then something happened – optimism in a time of tragedy, a perfect understanding of lack and need – what women lacked was diversion and what they needed were stockings.

Before the war as many as five-hundred-million pairs of silk stockings were sold annually in America, some women averaging fifty-five pairs in a year. With the scarcity of silk, it was the fancy mesh and very sheer dye-able cottons that rushed to popularity. All of a sudden there was color! 'As a rebellion to war, feet are stepping into gaiety', reported the *New York Post*.

"The heck with shortages," Mabel cried, "let's wear blue suede wedges with red piping and red stockings, and white mesh stockings with a red polished calf skin!"

New York was a bit startled when Mabel came out with a dancing shoe. In actuality, it was a version of the Chopine sandal which Charles designed, called the Pagan. Saks Fifth Avenue ran an ad in *The New Yorker*:

Specialists of the House #2: The Julianellis

'One night Charles whipped out a handful of ribbons and wound them around Mabel's tootsies, creating the Pagan sandal, which you have probably worn.'

The same *New Yorker* ad described Charles' determination to find ornaments for Mabel: 'Stationed in Cheyenne, Wyoming, he saw in a shop window a string of wooden beads made of two-toned Wyoming cedar and shipped a freight-car full of the cedar to Mabel, for buckles.'

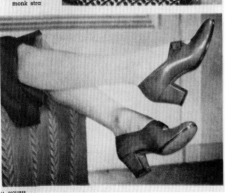

(Right) Blue nede lift with red piping: red on stockings. (Bew) White mesh stk-ings: red polied calf step-in wi a monk stra

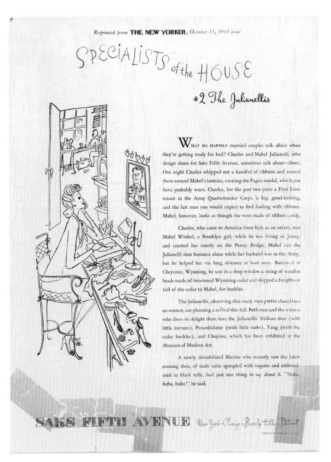

Far left: The cotton stocking companions: (top) Julianelli blue suede with red piping to accompany red cotton stockings; (bottom) red polished calf monk-strap with white mesh stockings, 1944. Unknown source.
Left: 'SFA Specialists of the House – The Julianellis', 1945. Saks Fifth Avenue ad in *The New Yorker*. Saks Fifth Avenue.

Mabel on the radio

She may have been speaking of dancing the nights away, but Mabel was lonely every night in her apartment on the river, longing to speak to Charles, and she thought grimly of the women bawling around her, Phyllis, Jeanne, her other sister-in-law Annette, Betty, and all the others – a nation-full.

One day Mabel volunteered to give shoe advice. She'd take a chance. She'd go in front of a radio microphone. She saw suddenly that women everywhere were like her, they were all crying. Nobody was dancing, not even Fred and Ginger, until the Chopine sandal from 1941 was back and it was raring to go. The women loved her, shyness and all.

'There are no men? So dance with each other!' Mabel told the readers of *The Philadelphia Inquirer*. 'We have made our Chopine for evening wear—okay, it's a sock, but what a sock, one to which you strap a very ornamental platform low or high-heeled sandal. For your lounging pant, you kick off the high-heel sandal. For dancing you kick off the low-heeled sandal. You then have a perfect shoe for your dancing dirndl, or your evening gown.

'I believe that national defense with its demands has had a good effect on fashion when we consider these new types of fabrication, or of decorations devised to compensate for the curtailment of metal gadgets used in the past. For those we have substituted appliqués of colored yarn, glass or amber beads. The bars are down,' she added. 'Anything goes to make a shoe!'

'Change your shoes three times a day!' Mabel said to the *Boston Globe*. 'Get yourself boudoir slippers that fit your feet! Don't scuff around in house-boats! It's not good for your feet or your morale! A good shoe lets you wiggle your toes.'

ABC Radio followed with Mabel's tidbits on its program, Fashion Flashes: "Buy the best shoes you can afford because leather today is a good investment," Mabel said. "Invest in the prettiest shoes, too, since there's no shortage of girl appeal."

'No shortage of *girl appeal*'—too flamboyant for a Flatbush girl? It turned out to be the best thing that Mabel said so far and the country loved her. Her 1944 phrase was quoted in Dallas' *Daily Times Herald*, in *The Philadelphia Inquirer*, in the *New York World-Telegram*, in Dayton, Ohio's *Journal*, to name a few. "If you're not born with beautiful feet, you can have them," Mabel vowed on *WOR*

What's afoot for summer?

Summer finds the Saks Shoe Salon full of
sparkling activity as usual . . . behind the scenes (here
you see one of our designers discussing a new
last with the Salon Director) as well as on stage.

Starred in our Summer stock: snow white
suedes, airy, immaculate; lightfooted pumps and
sandals, in bright black patent, and in
smooth black or brown suede. Plus our hit play shoes:
Raffiettes* our own brilliant successes;
platform sandals tied with gay scarves, colorful
rope sole sandals. (All these, and unrationed, too!)

*Reg. U. S. Pat. Off.   SHOE SALON, FOURTH FLOOR

ON THE COVER: Mink, natural and lustrous
in the new thirty-six inch coat. From an advance
Fall Collection. FUR SALON, FIFTH FLOOR

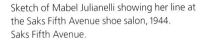

Sketch of Mabel Julianelli showing her line at
the Saks Fifth Avenue shoe salon, 1944.
Saks Fifth Avenue.

Radio, "An attractive, comfortable fitting pair of shoes can give girl appeal to any woman, and I can prove it!" Mabel knew before other designers how comfort and fashion could mesh.

A flood of women came to her office, and banged on the door of Room 850 in the Marbridge Building to find out how to get girl appeal and how to get it fast, radio microphones following them. Mabel, her hair painstakingly waved, her pale grey Norell suit flawless, her Julianelli pumps perfection, ran and hid behind Vincent, who hid behind Sam, when they saw the women coming.

But these women were so unhappy that Mabel loosened up and pushed Vincent and Sam aside and swiftly became the Jewish Mother Teresa of shoe advice. Now at that time, in wartime, the American press tended to portray American women either as jocks working in the ammunitions factories, or as pathetic wives and girlfriends, lost without their men. Mabel took these sentiments, lined them up, and readied them for extinction.

Mabel, who had suffered from shyness all her life, had found a peephole in time, an occasion to which she was able to rise, and she did it with a no-nonsense approach: "Well, well, well," Mabel said, "now you are sane women and you know you can't look well in every hat!"

Braced for an avalanche of raw nerves and tears, the radio commentators who were crammed into her little showroom with the newspaper reporters whispered among themselves.

"Why is she talking to those broads that way?" said one.

"Why is she talking about hats? Doesn't she make shoes?" said another.

"Ladies, a shoe is like a hat," continued Mabel, "it's infinite in color, shape and design. Even if a woman wears a size nine shoe, she can have a sexy foot if she has the proper shoe fitted to her foot. She should choose a shoe that lifts her instep up from the ground. This can be accomplished even in low-heeled shoes."

"Any woman whose feet are killing her, get up, if you can without falling, and march out of here," Mabel said. "There's no excuse for that."

Mabel advised her audience to listen to her on the radio every day. Finally smiles appeared on the faces of the women. Perhaps they liked her and she was doing something good. Women, sitting on the floor of her showroom, vented to her about living with the Program for National Defense's rationings, of curtailments, of reductions of goods and services, of life without their men.

"You don't think you deserve to be comfortable because your men aren't comfortable," Mabel said. "Well, well, well, you deserve to be comfortable, not to mention pretty!" She was starting to have a Louella Parsons-Hedda Hopper ring to her remarks. "They've called my shoes as important and exciting as a new vitamin or a swing ballad. Ladies, you can't wear a new vitamin or a swing ballad! But you can be comfortable in Julianellis."

"Any woman who must wear three-inch heels to work deserves what she gets when she cracks something in a street gutter. And I don't mean a bottle of champagne."

"Every shoe a woman slips into should be just as comfortable and easy as the husband she'll slip next to in bed when this crummy war is over."

Gossip columnist Hedda Hopper told listeners to her CBS radio program, The Hedda Hopper Show, that Mrs Julianelli's advice to women was as pithy as her own, and just as accurate.

These were full days, followed by empty nights, Mabel's loneliness expanding into a solitary dawn, which she tried to fill by writing Charles letters: 'I will see you July 15th at such time as you will knock on the door and say, 'Darling, it is your husband!' Ah, what a feeling comes over me – but it all seems like a dream now…I am waiting patiently for you to come home to me, for I am head over heels in love with you!'

New York was a city without men. Even the Marbridge Building was depleted except for the building manager, poor Mr D.S. Macdonald, and even he missed Charles. "It was a smart move of Charles' to go into the National Guard," he told Mabel. Manufacturers wrote to Charles. Mr J.G. Jones of the Rice-O'Neill Shoe Company of Saint Louis hoped Charles would not have to go very far 'before the thing is over'. These men could not serve and admired Charles for his youth and vigor. At the office, Sam and Vincent were the only pattern makers left. Leo and Eddie were stationed overseas. It felt like the family was all busted up.

An American patriot and a family man

Charles was happy in the Army. For the first time in sixteen years his hands got a rest from cutting patterns. If he were inclined to take stock of his life, now was the time, but for the moment he stuck strictly to the principles that defined his life, and in this new company of men, he continued to be an American patriot and a family man. Interestingly, on his enlistment record, he described his dependents as, 'mother, father and father-in-law', at a time when most men listed their wives. But Mabel was the bread-winner. In addition, unbeknown to him, she had turned their offices into a refuge for any woman needing her support.

"I know how it is for a fellow like yourself to leave your family and join Uncle Sam," Charles consoled a private.

"I hope this war will be over soon," the private said. "If we keep shellacking the enemy it won't be long before they crack. My brother has been classified 1A. Some have all the luck!"

"Here's my luck," Charles said, trying to be lighthearted. "I landed on KP duty the first day I got here. Felt like a steam roller rolled over me."

The private laughed, "How's your Mrs back home taking it?"

"She's taking it all right, well as can be expected," Charles shrugged.

When Mabel wasn't a camp follower, visiting Charles at Camp Upton in Long Island and later at Camp Lee in Virginia, where he attended Officer Candidate School, she was lonely beyond words. In the evenings she drowned herself in chocolate mousse from Horn & Hardart. On weekends she jumped at any chance to visit Charles' mother, and took her fill, with Annette and Jeanne, of Luigi's homemade wine.

The family was as anxious as the rest of the country while the men were away. Annette's husband, Jack Leyden, witnessed his carrier being nearly destroyed out in the North Pacific shooting down Japanese planes over Wake Island. Jeanne was about to follow her husband, Joe Azzariti, to California, where he was awaiting orders. Mabel, Annette and Jeanne comforted each other.

When Papa Winkel hung around her office Mabel was almost glad to see him, especially since he had outlived his political ardor and was almost kind to her. She sobbed so hard when lunching with Phyllis

Teschon in B. Altman & Co.'s Charleston Gardens, that she had to be carried out of the big room, done up in antebellum frescoes, like a tiny, teary-eyed Scarlett O'Hara. Going to the movies was impossible – *One Touch of Venus* and Mabel was bawling like a baby.

Mabel's pattern maker, Vincent, had a tendency to be jumpy around anything new or any new situation. But in this unusual climate, Vincent managed to be as uncharacteristic as possible and became Mabel's rock. In the evenings at the Thirty-Fifth Street entrance to the Marbridge Building, he waited in his car to take her home, trying as hard as he could not to cry.

"I'm sorry Signora," Vincent wailed, "but it is terrible Mr J. won't be home for Christmas."

"Maybe he'll get his furlough soon," Mabel cried.

Mabel encouraged the family to write to Charles often – Mama and Pop in Fairview, his mother's cousins, Armando and Isolina Gemignani from Union City, Annette and Jack Leyden from Baldwin, Long Island, Jeanne and Joe Azzariti from California, Aunt Katie and Uncle Alfred from Union City, Mabel's brother Ben Winkel from Naples, Florida, her cousin Anne Robinson and Anne's parents, Aunt Bertha and Uncle Will from Brooklyn, her sister Helen Davis, from Miami, Papa Winkel who had turned into a nice human being, and Vincent and Phyllis Teschon. The only distinct thing they had in common was the love they felt for Charles.

The times gained extra poignancy because Mabel did not have Charles to whom she could tell ideas. They were a team.

When she completed her design for a gold brocade clutch bag, she told the mailman. About her glove construction which she patented in 1945, she told the janitor. But it was commonly thought and she had to admit, that these inventions were dubious forms of nervous energy, filling the time until Charles came home.

'Then I will stay home and be your hostess, gloves, clutches, shoes be damned,' she wrote him. 'When you come home all the family will be waiting to see you and we will all rush up to you and give you kisses. It's a beautiful dream that I hope beyond anything comes true.'

Charles' furlough came in April and Mabel planned a family dinner. After dinner she washed the dishes with Phyllis, whose manner of jolliness implied that her husband Earle was home, and so he was, drinking too much homemade wine which came with Luigi. Mabel kept one eye on Charles in the living room, as the topic of Officer Candidate School came up. Mabel was inclined to think it odd for Charles to be pursuing a second career, and one in the Army, no less.

"It's a wonderful opportunity," said Phyllis.

"I'm glad he's going to school," whispered Mabel, "but only so he can be relieved of the responsibility of his folks. He deserves some freedom after all these years."

"So, what's the problem?"

"It's the state of Virginia, Phyllis. He'll be devoured by Southern Belles!"

Mabel did what she always did to forget any unpleasantness – she worked harder. She hired two little Italian finishers named Julia and Josephine, who spoke no English. Vincent was in Heaven. During the day and night shifts, the shop was a beehive; the men were going at it furiously, not only making shoe samples, but also bows and ornaments, for other manufacturers as well as Julianelli, out of any kind of cockamamie material that Mabel could find.

Mabel kept many large shoe factories working during this period. She was getting orders for hundreds of specialty bows and her unique leaf ornaments, or her two color leather twists. She made brass bound patterns and they were turned like a factory product, ten pairs at a time. Her ornaments were made of what she could find: from wire to candy wrappers.

Sam and Vincent worked at their lasts in one small room, and Mabel hired three more men to replace Leo and Eddie. At first, Julia and Josephine were frightened by the sight of so many men, and ran out of the office almost as soon as they walked in. But in time they settled down to the busy job of making shoe samples, bows and ornaments.

The office was filled with hundreds of yards of faille silk, and a couple of thousand dollars worth of beading. Mabel had lots of orders from manufacturers, including Frank Bros., Irving Florsheim, and I. Miller. No store promoted the Julianellis more than Saks Fifth Avenue; Saks was still their biggest fan.

Mabel came home on the train from camp in Virginia, with three wives who had husbands in Officer Candidate School. 'The wives whose husbands have been in for twelve weeks pull rank on the wives whose husbands have been in for nine weeks,' Mabel wrote to Charles, 'you should hear them, and the wives whose husbands have been in for nine weeks, ignore the wives of husbands in for five weeks. And we're all on the same train! That's the life we lead. And do you know that one of the wives told me that the official opinion is that the soldier who yells the loudest will make Commander? So yell, Darling.' Commander? She didn't want Charles to be a Commander.

The graduation was in August, 1944, in Petersburg, Virginia. Mabel planned to buy Charles' uniform at Saks Fifth Avenue, but the salesman said the Brigadier General had been waiting four weeks for

Opposite: Saks Fifth Avenue sketch of Mabel Julianelli at shoe salon, when Charles was in the Army, 1944. Saks Fifth Avenue.

A pump for town-wear worn by the ladies who were often seen lunching at Schrafft's. Leather cable-lace ending in a gold-hued bit buckle, mid-heel: 2½ inches, 1960. Photograph by John Manno.

Mabel was one of the first to work with faux reptile, shown here for a pump with a cross-stem ornament, mid-heel: 2½ inches, 1960. Photograph by John Manno.

his. Mabel bought one from a shoe salesman who knew a tailor and sent it to Charles to have it fitted. She went with Mama Onorata, Annette and Jeanne to the graduation ceremony and at the last minute asked Phyllis to join her in case she got upset and needed her. Mabel would not be jealous; she had rehearsed a thousand times and gathered all her reserve in order to cope with seeing Charles, wearing the uniform she bought for him, surrounded by drooling Southern Belles. She could smell their heavy perfume and hair tonic, but as she approached him to pin on his First Lieutenant Bars, they cleared away.

Mabel dreamed about Charles walking into Saks Fifth Avenue with his Bars on, and about showing him off to the men at the office. She tried not to get out of hand over his rapid rise in the Army. She had the fear the Army would take him away from her for good, and she had the distinct certainty that Charles was not happy in the shoe business.

He wasn't coming home but going into the Army Quartermaster Corps in Cheyenne, Wyoming. "Remember, Dear," she cried at the train platform in Petersburg, "when you have to give a command, shout with all your might and you may just make Commander. Make a lot of noise. Think of the enemy sticking a bayonet into a good American boy and shout like Hell!" Secretly, all she really wanted was for them to go to a double feature together and eat coffee ice cream at Schrafft's.

Charles smoked the pipe Mabel gave him, and read her letter: 'It was wonderful to be with you again. Each time I come home I seem more filled with your goodness and love. It all seems so strange seeing you in uniform, snatching minutes together. You are so steady and sure of yourself. I always want to see you that way. I have felt strong and good inside – full of your good love.'

A few months went by. Over a butterscotch sundae sprinkled with whole salted almonds, the women went about their favorite pastime: being catty at Schrafft's. Mabel sat between Cousin Isolina and her daughter Rina, mentally recording any of their stinging quips to write in her letters to Charles. Charles didn't miss a thing that happened in Jersey or Schrafft's.

'They were very high-hat since Rina's truck driver husband is a First Lieutenant,' Mabel wrote. 'Rina blurted, "I'm having a baby," and Isolina turned to Jeanne and said, "I cannot understand why you don't have one." That hurt Jeanne. I guess if you're married to a truck driver, you become as mean as a truck.' Mabel ended her letter to Charles with: 'Gee, darling, we've got to get that baby soon.'

March 9, 1959

The flight to India started in Rome the afternoon before, at 2:05 pm, due to arrive in Istanbul at 7:05 pm, with a three-hour stopover. The Julianellis left Istanbul at 10:30 pm, and did not arrive in New Delhi until 3:05 pm the following day. They would be away from home for five weeks, beginning the trip with a week in Paris, and returning home to Idlewild Airport, after their stay in India, via Rome, Milan and Paris.

Mabel toyed a moment with the little curtain, and drew it across the Aegean Sea. Back in the distance was the Ashoka Hotel in New Delhi, with the beautiful women in saris and the men in turbans.

The Julianellis were assigned a young boy in an orange turban and white suit. He took care of all their needs while they were at the hotel. Their room was filled with flowers which he brought every day. They met maharajas and maharani. Mabel wrote home about 'the variance of dress between the Sheiks, warriors of old, and the Hindus and the Moslems,' and of 'rubies, emeralds and sapphires dripping all over the place.'

But Charles did not seem well. He was smoking too much. Mabel found him on one occasion in the Ashoka lounge, wearing a Raijput headdress, worn by the Indian Armed Forces, sharing a smoke with other similarly turbaned men.

Oh, the joys, the sorrows, the saris of India! It had been a mixed adventure and marked a moment when Mabel took stock of her accomplishments. It was true, she was a pip-squeak, just like her father said she was — tiny yet pushy, blasting through the design monopoly of the shoe manufacturers to establish herself as 'the Lady Shoe Designer', the name Vincent gave her. Who were her peers when she burst onto the scene in 1929? Herman Delman had been designing in America, and Salvatore Ferragamo in Italy. Mabel had been running her own shoe business before David Evins changed his career from fashion illustrator to shoes, and before Beth Levine was designing for I. Miller. Mabel Julianelli had led the way for designers, for women and for pip-squeaks.

Dreams of being a mother

One night in September, 1945, when she was sitting alone, aching over the fact that First Lieutenant Charles Julianelli was in the Army Quartermaster Corps, in Cheyenne, Wyoming, as she listened to Burns and Allen, the moon's reflection vying with the neon billboard to cast the brightest luster on the river, Mabel knew she was pregnant.

It was a boy. Mabel named him Emmanuel. He was not healthy, in fact, quite sickly, but to her, he was the most beautiful baby in the world. Charles was ecstatic. He had come home briefly when Emmanuel was born, but Mabel was alone as her baby slipped away, and not understanding the medical reasons, she was hysterical. Just before Charles came home for good, Emmanuel died, and with him, all her warm dreams of being a mother, giving a son to Charles, a grandson to Onorata, Luigi, and Papa Winkel, a nephew to Annette and Jeanne, a godchild to Phyllis and to Vincent. In her shame of losing the baby, Mabel was sure she had lost them all too, the moment her little boy was put in the grave.

January, 1946. Charles was home, and there was a good deal of euphoria about. During the first post-war fashion season there was enormous productivity going on in the postage-stamp sample factory of Julianelli Inc., with Charles drawing, Vincent cutting and gluing, Sam, Leo and Eddie cutting and singing, and Julia and Josephine finishing. In the showroom, Phyllis was modeling, and in the reception room, Jeanne was filing and Betty was typing. Everyone was home and everyone was happy. Mabel, in the front office, moved by an excited frenzy, announced that anyone working for her had to step up the pace, somewhat ill-timed when almost every married woman in America was pregnant and about to hatch the Baby Boom generation.

But step up the pace they did, even Mabel's own pregnant Phyllis and Betty. The newspaper columnists and magazine editors reported daily on the trend-setting Julianelli originals: 'an amazing number of stunning styles', one reporter wrote, cranked out of the tiny rooms in the Marbridge Building. It wasn't all euphoria. There was always someone stupid lurking around.

One trap Mabel fell right into; a reporter for a Midwestern newspaper asked her at a press conference, "You're a married couple, right?"

"Yes," said Mabel, who happened to be without Charles that day.

Opposite: In love and in business, 1948.

S.F.A. puts a famous
GLOVE FABRIC *on your* **FEET**

Elvette* cloth—now in glove-soft, glove-light shoes. Shoes with a new handling—shirred, draped, these even embroidered in tiny beads. From an exclusive Julianelli designed collection, 27.95. Fourth Floor. Matched Elvette* bag, 52.50** and gloves, 7.50. Street Floor.   *Reg. **Sub. to Fed. Tax

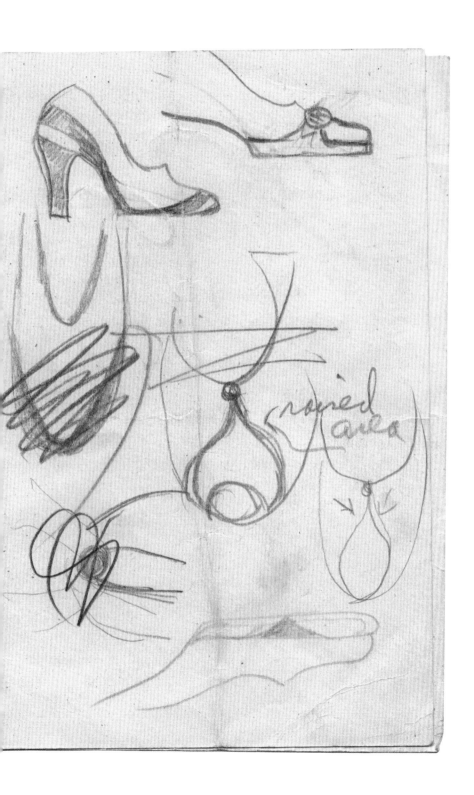

This page: Mabel Julianelli for Julianelli Inc. Sketches including the *Lilt* construction (upper left), 1948. © 2010 Jane Julianelli.
Opposite: Saks Fifth Avenue advertisement for glove-soft Elvette cloth on Julianelli collection, 1946. Saks Fifth Avenue.

"Why do you produce so many shoes? Is it because you're afraid to produce a baby because it would be nothing more than a —" Here the man used two ethnic slurs.

"Listen," Mabel said, as the man was escorted out of Room 850 by Vincent and Sam, "when my beautiful baby is born, I'll be sure you get the picture."

Fashion reversed itself all the time. One minute the Julianellis designed a shoe which was held fast to the ankle by a dozen jet buttons, the next a shoe whose buttons did nothing useful, simply cascaded down the heel. Another Julianelli trend was a closed toe-and-heel pump, smart with the Empire-derived dresses. Next came a bared foot with a low-cut instep called the Little T, also inspired by the Empire shoes of Napoleon and Josephine.

The Julianelli construction, the Lilt, was worn on pumps at Sardi's. The Lily pad heel construction was seen on a dancing sandal at the Rainbow Room. Mabel foresaw the coming of mass pre-natal backache, and emphasized her open-sided, low-heeled shoe in fabrics, leathers and faux reptile, which was suitable for afternoon, evening, and morning sickness.

Saks Fifth Avenue was with them all the way, calling each Julianelli innovation, no matter how different, 'Very Saks Fifth Avenue', from Ecclesiastical Moyen Age Brocade evening slippers, to their pre-historic plant and animal painted buckles on platform shoes.

Mabel and Charles produced shoe designs, shoe shows and shoe advice. Columnist Berta Mohr quoted Mabel on the subject of comfort in Toronto's *Star Weekly:* 'Buy your shoes large enough, especially if they have closed toes, unless you want to risk bunions, nervous discomfort, and worse, dislocations.

'Apply this rule: look at the soles of your old shoes. If the worn part is only in the front, and the back part of the sole is unscuffed you are pushing too far forward and need a longer size. In a properly fitted shoe, your heel rests firmly on the center of the shoe's heel. If the shoe heel is too far forward, or too far back on the foot, you ruin the shoe and your disposition.'

In the 1947 Saks Fifth Avenue fashion show, shoe designers Ferragamo of Florence and Julianelli were the two featured in Saks' first collection after the war, presented in the Louis Sixteenth Suite of the St Regis Hotel. Given a formal opening as befitted a collection of paintings, the emphasis was on the shoe as art, in the Italian Ferragamos and, as Alice Hughes in the *Times Herald* put it: 'our own native Julianellis'. *Women's Wear Daily* reported: 'The guests of honor were Charles and Mabel Julianellis, who are responsible for many of this store's original designs.'

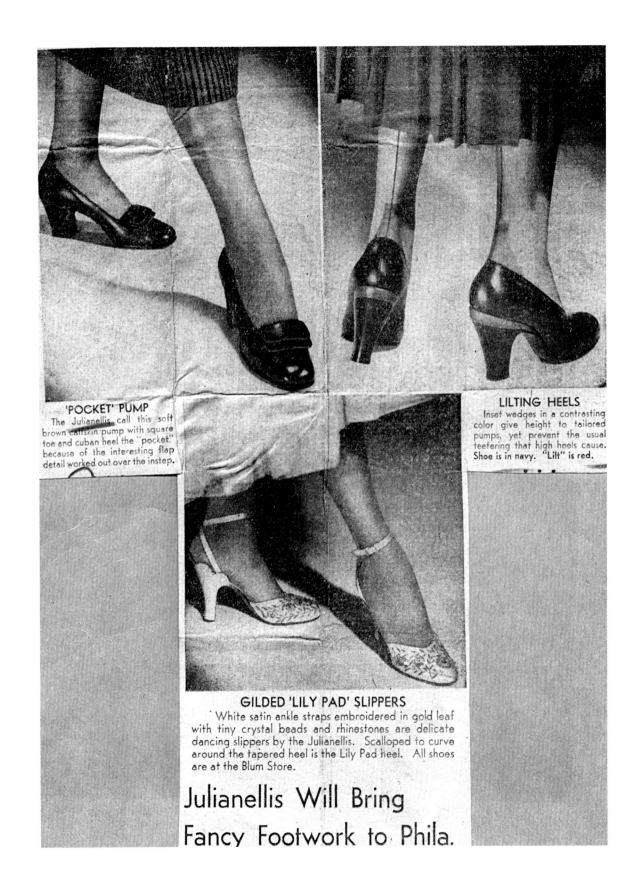

'POCKET' PUMP
The Julianellis call this soft brown calfskin pump with square toe and cuban heel the "pocket" because of the interesting flap detail worked out over the instep.

LILTING HEELS
Inset wedges in a contrasting color give height to tailored pumps, yet prevent the usual teetering that high heels cause. Shoe is in navy. "Lilt" is red.

GILDED 'LILY PAD' SLIPPERS
White satin ankle straps embroidered in gold leaf with tiny crystal beads and rhinestones are delicate dancing slippers by the Julianellis. Scalloped to curve around the tapered heel is the Lily Pad heel. All shoes are at the Blum Store.

Julianellis Will Bring Fancy Footwork to Phila.

The Julianellis began to invent some of their best shoe constructions since the prolific 1930s. Why should a woman teeter in her heels? And the 1948 Julianelli Lilt inset filled a woman's need. The heel started lower, the arch stayed high. Why should a woman not feel secure when dancing in her open sandal? The Julianelli Lily Pad construction was invented to do away with the gap above the heel and part of the shank with the addition of a scalloped silhouette in dancing shoes.

Because buckles fell off, and there were still few materials with which to make them, Mabel invented a new form of shoe decoration called the Shoestring Square. The shoe was cut deep to the toe with an insert of suede in colors, under a crossed shoe string.

The country's taste and preference for shoes always differed vastly, from the Northeast to the Southwest, so that even if the Julianellis found one side of the nation loved Mae West, and the other, Lauren Bacall, they still had to design for both, with Doris Day in the middle.

Lord & Taylor, in one of their first Julianelli ads in the *New York Herald Tribune*, promoted the 1948 classic Julianellis, including the Pyramid, a black suede pump with a standup suede and rhinestone buckle, the Little T, and the Baroque, an ankle-strap with a figure eight cut-out on the vamp. Baltimore's Hess advertised them too. The Blum Store of Philadelphia chose to feature a Julianelli caned-leather shoe. The first store in the Southwest to flip over the daintiness of Julianelli's 'high-stepping' sling-backs was Volk of Dallas, advertising them in the *Daily Times Herald* and the *Dallas Morning News*.

Original shoe constructions and signature details, 1948: (left) the Bootee in black suede with three-buttons; (middle) the Lily Pad construction, scallop curved around heel, this one embroidered in gold leaf and tiny crystal beads and rhinestones; (right) Shoestring Square décor, insert of suede behind crossed shoe strings to replace with other inserts of leather or fabric. Unknown source.

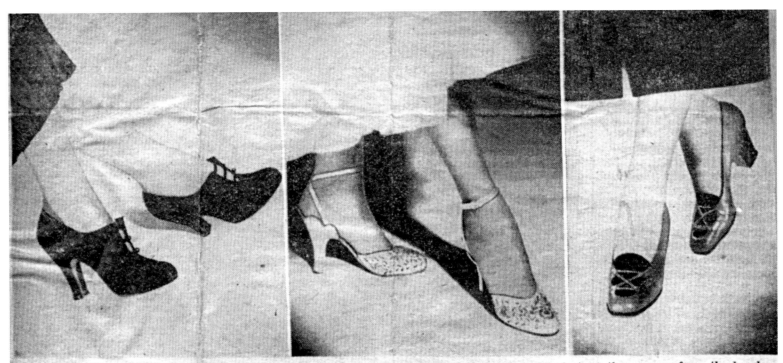

VARIETY is the spice of life, in shoes, too, and here are three of the latest designs for milady's feet, as they appear from the bench of Mabel and Charles Julianelli. At left is the "Bootie" a sleek town shoe of the three-button boot type in black suede. Center photo is a white satin ankle strap number called "Lily Pad," embroidered in gold leaf with tiny crystal beads and rhinestones, with lily pad heel, scalloped to curve around heel. On right is a new form of shoe decor, an insert of brown suede to replace decorations that are always falling off. This shoe is of rust calfskin and is called "Shoestring Square."—(Int.)

To keep ahead the Julianellis were always designing. Charles designed the Aboriginal, a footprint sandal. He took an actual impression of the foot on a piece of wet leather, which he molded up around the instep and tied with leather thongs. Mabel came up with a straw shoe in the winter of 1948, which was in the stores by April 1949, featured in the December issue of *Harper's Bazaar*. It was one trend among many that was copied by other shoe companies – biscuit-colored straw sandals, heightened into dressy shoes with high heels, a straw mule, a straw pump trimmed with leather or faille silk, or simulated bamboo.

Alice Hughes' ode to Julianelli in April's 'New York Report' for Dallas' *Daily Times Herald* read: 'Always the beautiful instep arch, the slender ankle, the Patrician prance of a beautifully shod foot are apparent in full nakedness beneath the delicate tracer of thin strips and latticework.'

'Achieving a style-setting 'first' in the fashion world is the aim of all shoe designers, and New York's Mr. and Mrs. Julianelli have chalked up style leaders almost every season in the last few years,' wrote Berta Mohr in the April, 1949 issue of *The Star Weekly*.

"Here she goes again," said Vincent, as he watched Mabel examining the traffic-splashed ankles of his wife and mother-to-be, little Josephine, one of the finishing women. "We'll design something to protect those feet – we'll design you a Bootee," exclaimed the concerned Mabel.

"I don't think Italian women wear Bootees, do they?" ventured Sam.

"My Josephine will wear Bootees if Mrs J tells her to!" Vincent blanched to defend her.

"What are Bootees?" asked Leo.

If they had imagined knitted baby booties, they were a thousand miles in the wrong direction – these were sassy high-top patent leather and suede boots. And when Mabel and Charles launched them they were so hot that newspapers reporting on them had to refer to the Civil War and your granny's old-fashioned button hook to cool their effect. And who took a fancy to them? Everyone.

The Bootee town shoe had three buttons, and the Spat boot climbed to an eight-button height. Referred to as 'Good Mudders' or 'High Climbers' in California's *Register-Pajaronian,* they were

Opposite: Exclusives for Lord & Taylor, 1948. Lord & Taylor.

These are the shoes of

Mabel and Charles Julianelli _

now ours alone.

Shoes of perfect, fine-drawn proportions

with taper toes and

thin, delicate heels.

18.95 to 20.95 (rhinestone buckle extra)

On the Fourth Floor

Also at Manhasset and Westchester

termed 'a fun-producing fashion revival, a good 'go-with' for long street skirts,' by Elmira, New York's *Star-Gazette*. The ankle-high leather boots were functional on the outside, but inside, Mabel's shock effect came out – a lining of bright red satin, which worked for women everywhere.

Dorothy Roe, fashion editor for *Associated Press*, wrote animatedly about the Julianelli high button boots both in the *Oakland Tribune* and Nebraska's *Lincoln Sunday Journal and Star* with the headline: Dictators of Styles Predict High Button Shoes Next Fall! 'This quiet, hard-working young couple has become virtual dictators of America's feminine shoe styles. For next fall and winter the Julianellis already have made a number of models, guaranteed to startle the public and recall the halcyon days of *Godey's Lady's Book*' (a lady's publication from the Civil War).

Mabel told Dorothy Roe: 'The shoe mode for next season is going to run to two extremes—high, boot types or extremely open styles.' As Mabel thought back to poor Josephine's wet feet, she said with satisfaction, 'The street versions will be spat types that save a woman's feet, with suede uppers and water repellent patent leather bottoms.'

It's not certain who first coined the phrases 'barely any shoe at all' or 'held on by a string' to describe the Julianelli evening sandals of 1949; it might have been Alice Hughes. And if it was not Hughes, it was surely Eleanor Lambert.

Empress of fashion, fashion publicist, promoter of American fashion, originator of the International Best-Dressed List, founder of the Council of Fashion Designers of America – Eleanor Lambert fell in love with Mabel Julianelli.

Nearly choking on her chef salad in the Plaza Hotel's Palm Court after hearing a beefy Katharine Hepburn accent emerge from a tiny, buxom lady at the next table: "My dear... if...the SHOE isn't RIGHT, why then, the whole costume is RUINED," Lambert had to meet Julianelli. Eleanor Lambert signed up the Julianellis immediately. Lambert was most impressed with Mabel Julianelli's ingenuity, glove-like fitting shoes, and good taste in husbands.

"I always hoped he'd come through an officer," Mabel told Lambert about Charles, "for our public."

"I bet he looks good out of uniform too," Lambert replied.

Listening to Lambert go crazy over them during a dinner at Henri Soulé's posh eatery, Le Pavillon, Mabel and Charles knew they had found their pot of gold. Lambert had created the annual Coty Fashion Critics Awards, which were the Oscars of the fashion industry. With one of her quotes:

Low Heel Series

Ornaments   Leaf

Colonial

Bootee

Closed & open to Dressy Oxfords

Mabel Julianelli for Julianelli Inc. Sketches of the Low Heel Series, and Josephine's lace-in-back Bootee or Spat (third row), leaf ornament (top row), 1949. © 2010 Jane Julianelli.

'The fashion industry waits for the Julianelli styles before the season can successfully start,'

Lambert brought the Julianelli trademark to the rest of the world, as she had done for American designers, Norman Norell, Oscar de la Renta, Bill Blass, and artist, Isamu Noguchi.

From her office at 785 Fifth Avenue, Lambert applauded the Julianellis. If a press release regarding keynotes of famous American designers was sent from her office, Mabel and Charles Julianelli were quoted with Hattie Carnegie, Adele Simpson, Adrian, Lily Daché and Pauline Trigère. If a newspaper published predictions of leading designers, Mabel and Charles Julianelli were included with Nettie Rosenstein, Norman Norell, Claire McCardell and Ben Reig.

But Lambert admonished them too, "You must see Italy and France or you cannot be full designers." After that they traveled, to Paris, Rome, Milan, and Bologna. They did not go to Charles' native Lucca. He wanted to take his mother back one day. Mabel promised they would make it the very next trip.

Straight from the Army, Charles went back full time into pattern cutting and design, playing with an original idea, a new handling, a new shirring, or embroidery. When he faltered Mabel coaxed him, "The Coty Award isn't far away." He had heard of the Coty Award, something every fashion designer dreamed of, yet the words were as foreign as his mother's words, "America isn't far away," to a little boy on a ship bound for an unknown destination, and just as unimaginable.

The Julianellis designed hundreds of samples. The Marbridge Building swelled with shoe buyers, fashion designers, press, wholesalers and retailers, everyone grabbing for the shoes. People said hello to Mabel whom she never saw in her life. There was such an abundance of clippings, photographs and articles, that Mabel moved Julia and Josephine from their finishing table and hired another woman to cut clippings full time. Mabel bought a white bookcase that covered the wall behind her desk and lined it with scrapbooks. The look was Julianelli, and in the fashion business the question of the day was 'Do Your Feet Have This Look?'

Julianelli Back Interest
Oppsite top: Signature back interest with double buckled strap (left); (right) Lily Pad construction: satin evening slipper, beaded in crystal and rhinestones, daintily scalloped in black to hug slim heels for dancing, both 1948. As seen in US *Harper's Bazaar*.
Opposite middle: Backswept, signature back interest, rhinestone buckle at heel, black satin back, black suede front, 1949. Unknown source
Opposite bottom: Sketch of a satin pump with the Julianelli signature back interest and elongated vamp construction, designed for Fashions of the Times, 1950. Unknown source.

Alice Huges, who took them very seriously, wrote in her 'A Woman's New York' column for the *Tribune*, 'Too Few Shoe Designers: All of us in the fashion racket can run off dozens of names of dress designers, milliners, jewelry, and textile designers. But shoe designers' names do not spring so quickly to mind. To be sure there are numbers of shoe manufacturers and someone designs their shoes. But for some reason their names are not publicized. Some shoe firm heads design their own, or else take credit for the shoes brought out under their names. But as for actual designers who specialize only in creating new shoe styles each season, one of the few names that comes to mind is that of the Julianellis.'

"She's so serious about us, you must take her to lunch," said Mabel to Charles.

"You should go," said Charles, "I recall she liked your pompadour at the Barberry."

Mabel and Alice Hughes managed lunch one day at Schrafft's on Seventy-Ninth Street, Mabel's turf, where she could feel comfortable lunching with a very big reporter. The discussion turned to family trees. Taking no chances, Mabel invented her pedigree on the spot, over-playing a gesture with her butterscotch-and-almond-heaped spoon: "Oh, did you know I'm related to Rembrandt Von Rijn?"

"I was referring to the future of your family tree," responded Hughes, "anyone in the making?"

"THE BACKSWEPT" pump in black suede and satin has a rhinestone buckle in back; $22.95.

Mabel said she could only wish for a child. Eventually – and Hughes got the scoop – Mabel became pregnant again. A daughter was born. The poor little creature seemed to have been put on the earth solely to endow Mabel with the inspiration to design children's shoes, and give endless children's shoe advice to every columnist remotely interested in children: 'We never planned to go into infant's shoes, but to make Janie's shoes has become a labor of love,' Mabel said to Alice Hughes in the *Telegram*. 'And of course, it's only natural that we name a new baby shoe for her. It's been put on the market in many stores.'

Closed Back for Beige Satin

In 1949 Mabel saw the return of her wartime audience, this time as new mothers. Again she was all the rage and an easy touch for any mother with a complaint about an aching back, aching arches, or aching toddlers, and for a time, Mabel was close to being signed for a *WOR Radio* talk show of her own. "...And we are against support for children's feet because nature supplies the muscles and bones that make for good feet so support grows where it is needed," Doctor Mabel said on *WOR Radio*. "And we feel strongly on the subject of soft-sole shoes for children – in fact for everybody. The old-time parental theory that stiff leather shoes are better for children because they last longer is a mistaken one. For most children's feet outgrow their shoes in size faster than they can out-wear the leather."

"And every child, we feel, should have at least one pair of red shoes," Mabel said. "It's good for their eyes to see the brightness."

"When I'm on the air discussing bad infant footwear versus good infant footwear, do you listen to me?" Mabel asked Charles one evening in bed.

"Of course, your voice is so mesmerizing," Charles said humorously, as he dozed into his pillow." He liked to play with her because he knew his wife, and when the novelty of children's shoes wore off, there would be no time for anything but designing grown-up shoes.

Vincent was now a happy man. He did not complain that they were making children's shoes because he was a father. Divested of his loneliness, Vincent became a changed man. And so did Charles; fatherhood was ideal for him.

His little girl, with black hair like the color he once had, his button nose, his eyes and his eyebrows, was Mabel all the way,

a mischief who went in heavily for pranks and theatrics at home, yet remained shy in the outside world. And just like Mabel, she relied on Charles to protect her.

The pull of recognition was so conflicting for an introvert like Mabel, that at times, while luring her forward, it drew her back to the lonely little rascal she once was, and she prayed that her only child would never endure her earlier grief. So, shortly after Mabel's daughter was born, when Annette and

Jack had a baby boy, John, and Jeanne and Joe had a baby girl, Ona, it seemed her prayers had been answered, and that the three cousins would grow up playing together, even if only on Sundays.

Leading up to 1950, Julianelli Inc. with their shoes manufactured locally in the Zuckerman & Fox factory in New York City, designed for almost every high-end store from New York to California, giving exclusivity to many on certain groupings of shoes. The Julianellis criss-crossed the country, often traveling separately because of the baby, making appearances in the salons of the Smart Shop in Houston, Lord & Taylor and Bonwit Teller in New York, Hess in Baltimore, Krupp & Tuffly's in Houston, Volk Bros. in Dallas, Himelhoch's in Detroit, and Blum Store in Philadelphia.

Mabel traveled without Charles for a public appearance at Joseph Salon Shoes in Chicago. In a nearby hotel a bristly front desk clerk took one look at Mabel and stated that her reservation had been canceled, escorting her to the door. Though her name was Italian, Mabel's face was Semitic, with characteristics of the faces of Jewish Russians and Poles, originally from Eastern Europe, known as Displaced Persons, who had recently become very noticeable in Chicago.

Mabel knew instinctively what the front desk man meant. She wished she had responded to him with an answer that she only thought of later: "You reject me for my birth and for my starting point, but I have worked hard, because of both and in spite of both, to be the woman I am today." Instead, returning home in tears, Mabel suffered in silence, though felt proud she was Jewish. But despite her Italian name, was it so obvious?

Mabel never told Charles about the incident, but focused on the importance of shoes in a 1949 season of changeless silhouettes when the Fashion League reported on the big part played by the cut of a shoe. The Julianelli Inc. production machine was quickly devouring the Julianellis in constant media visibility and non-stop store appearances. They were photographed, sketched, and caricatured. Mabel did not want to travel in the States without Charles, because of experiences like the incident in Chicago. She believed that the gentile appearance of Charles would put an end to it, which it did when he went with her.

Volk Bros., a leading specialty store in Dallas virtually adopted the Julianellis and took credit for their start in the Southwest. In a full-page *Footwear News* editorial, called 'How Volk's Sold a Name', they outlined in rather cowboy fashion just how they did it, step by step. An approximation was: 'Bring 'em in. Handle 'em with care!' It continued: 'Sell the exclusive Julianelli franchise with careful planning and showmanship. Acquaint the public relations director with Julianelli's styling and arrange a public appearance. Officially announce the Julianelli line in Dallas newspaper ads to

Top: Strappy mule for Saks Fifth Avenue, 1949.
Bottom: Mule for Saks Fifth Avenue, 1949.

Team Mabel and Charles, 1949.

coincide with Dallas fall fashion presentations in leading stores, and attempt to secure one-hundred-and thirty-nine inches of editorial space. President Harold F. Volk will send five-thousand invitations to meet the Julianellis.'

It was a grueling three-day promotion, a press showing on Monday afternoon, cocktails with the press and Mr Volk at night, Tuesday morning, a meeting with the Volk customers, a radio broadcast interview, and a return to the store and another meeting on Wednesday.

From the moment it began, the Julianellis realized that it was the intention of every key store in every key American city to adopt them, and to take credit for their start. So they had many starts in many places. But of all their promoters Volk Bros. was the most colorful, declaring in one *Dallas Morning News* ad: 'What the halter dress does for the girl—the halter shoe does for her foot. We see these two shoes inspiring oh's and ah's along with the new afternoon crepes! Both, good Texas shoes—where we only have about two weeks of 'yankee winter'. Means glamour at your feet the year-round.' Julianelli's ladylike sensibility was attracting the entire country.

Mabel championed the naked foot, beginning in the 1940s, and initiated the era's chain craze with her bare chain. Chain ankle strap sandal, 1950

Partying with the fashion elite

Over the Julianellis, the intoxication of fame was fluidly spreading. Mabel broke the 'rule' that bare shoes were appropriate only for spring and summer. She broke another 'rule' that it was the tailored shoe alone that went with textured stockings. She always preferred textured stockings with a round-heeled lightweight pump.

With Charles to shield her and Eleanor Lambert to guide her, Mabel Julianelli never declined a request for an appearance in or out of town. At Eleanor Lambert's Jubilee Show of New York Fashions, the Julianellis brought the house down with their rhinestone Little T t-strap. On automobile wheels, the Julianellis were presented at the General Motors' Wheel of Fashion show, another inspiration of Ms Lambert's. There were showings at *The New York Times* Fashion Show, and Lord & Taylor's fashion shows at the Bird Cage luncheon room, where all of the odd, uncomfortable little seats with welded table trays were pushed back to make space for a miniature runway.

They attended shows in which Julianelli Shoes were featured at the National Shoe Retailers Association Style Conference at the Ritz-Carlton Hotel, the International Silk Association's World of Silk fashion show for the benefit of the US Committee for the United Nations International Children's Emergency Fund (UNICEF). A fashion show for the benefit of the Women's American ORT, whose name came from the Russian society for trades and agricultural labor, helped them provide financial support to Eastern European Jews. These last two events both took place at the Waldorf Astoria Hotel and were presented by Eleanor Lambert. Julianelli shoes accessorized Texan designer Tom Brigance's Spring into Summer show at the New York Athletic Club, and the American Bankers Association Luncheon and Fashion Show at the Hotel Commodore, presented by The New York Dress Institute, of which Eleanor Lambert was director.

Most often there was a traditional fashion show, but then somebody would throw a party and mislabel it an industry event when it was more like a wild sorority jubilee, or some jolly production of skits that privileged fraternity boys performed for parent's weekend – a sort of carefree, devil-may-care, throw-caution-to-the-wind evening of merriment. The party was always for a good cause, and exploding with famous people.

One of the best parties, year after year, was held in a new wing of the Metropolitan Museum of Art called the Costume Institute. It was aptly called the Party of the Year.

The Julianelli Permanent Collection at The Metropolitan Museum of Art: The Costume Institute
Opposite: (Sandals); Black Satin and Crepe; Silk; Spike heel; Late 1950s to early 1960s. The Metropolitan Museum of Art, Gift of Mabel Julianelli, 1973 (1973.23.1). Image © The Metropolitan Museum of Art.
Next page left: (Strip sandals); Gold Kid; Ankle Straps; Late 1950s to early 1960s. The Metropolitan Museum of Art, Gift of Mabel Julianelli, 1973 (1973.23.1). Image © The Metropolitan Museum of Art.
Next page right: (Pumps); Closed; Embroidered; Metallic; beads and sequins; Late 1950s to early 1960s. The Metropolitan Museum of Art, Gift of Mabel Julianelli, 1973 (1973.23.1). Image © The Metropolitan Museum of Art.

The Julianelli Permanent Collection at The Metropolitan Museum of Art: The Costume Institute

Previous spread left: (Pumps); Gold Kid; Embroidered; Bronze beads; imitation topaz jewels; Snipped Toe; Late 1950s to early 1960s. The Metropolitan Museum of Art, Gift of Mabel Julianelli, 1973 (1973.23.1). Image © The Metropolitan Museum of Art.
Previous spread right: (Pumps); Closed; Bronze Satin; Bronze beads; Snipped Toe; late 1950s to early 1960s. The Metropolitan Museum of Art, Gift of Mabel Julianelli, 1973 (1973.23.1). Image © The Metropolitan Museum of Art.

From the first Party of the Year in 1948, which was sponsored by members of the fashion industry for the maintenance of the Costume Institute, the Julianellis were among the contributors and the revelers. Charles saw that although the party was for charity, for one night a year it helped him and people like him, working in the fashion industry, ease the daily ordeal of dressing American women.

At the third annual Party of the Year there was a theatre-in-the-round production called *Love's Young Dream*, introduced by Lord & Taylor president, Dorothy Shaver, starring Betsy Von Furstenberg dressed in Anne Fogarty. There were grab bags with prizes worth up to one thousand dollars, photographers Dahl-Wolfe, Horst, Milton Greene and Scavullo on hand to take a picture, and dinner.

One of the biggest extravaganzas was the March of Dimes fashion show, Scenes of Spring, presented by the New York Dress Institute Couture Group, produced by Eleanor Lambert at the Waldorf-Astoria Hotel. If one were lucky or talented enough to attend this benefit for the National Foundation for Infantile Paralysis, one would have been treated to stage décor by Cecil Beaton and Alexander Calder, opening remarks by Helen Hayes, a script by Anita Loos, music by Lester Gaba, commentaries by Sir Cedric Hardwicke, Arthur Treacher, Yvonne Adair, Peter Lind Hayes and Mary Healey, Celeste Holm and Katharine Hepburn. The fashion show featured designers Hattie Carnegie, Christian Dior, Jacques Fath, Mollie Parnis, Ben Reig, Trigère, Claire McCardell, Tom Brigance, Adele Simpson, with many of their outfits accessorized by Julianelli shoes.

It seemed that wherever Eleanor Lambert was, there was a party. It was all fun and New York loved it. The Julianellis were part of the fashion elite, always honored and respected. But outside New York their treatment could be most cavalier: 'Meet the Julianellis, husband and wife designer team!' was the cry from Blums in Philadelphia. 'See Charles who makes the samples. See him in the lobby window turning and stitching unique shapes into leather!'

One promotion manager thought it was a good idea to put Charles Julianelli in a store window like a performing circus clown. The window was hotter than Philly in summer, as Chestnut Street outside filled with inquisitive people who wondered what Charles was doing as he looked so pathetic; soon they left, embarrassed at being asked to be voyeurs. Charles was perspiring under hot spot lights, and the accelerated routine of sketching, cutting, turning and stitching made him look like a wooden puppet doing wooden functions as an invisible puppeteer cranked his wooden handle.

The next time the Julianellis went to Blums in Philadelphia, Charles brought Leo their cobbler along to demonstrate how to make a sample. Leo delighted in the presence of an audience to watch him work, and hear him sing in Italian.

Above: Rhinestone ankle strap version of evening sandal, 1949.
Opposite: Mules, flats and sandals, 1950. As seen in US *Harper's Bazaar.*

BRIGHT MULES AND

1. In velvet, the new sandal-mule—a mule with a T-strap in front with three crossbars. About $25.
2. The evening flat in deep purple velvet, its T-strap glinting with artificial amethysts. About $25.
3. The network sandal—strips of kid with diamond shapes of kid forming a T-strap. About $35.
4. Seen in profile and in black velvet this time, the evening flat described in Number 2. All the shoes shown on this page are by Julianelli, winner of a 1950 special American Fashion Critics' Award sponsored by Coty. All are available at Lord and Taylor; Julius Garfinckel; Harzfeld's; Himelhoch.

Eugenia Sheppard, an important friend

Back in New York Eugenia Sheppard, syndicated fashion columnist for *The New York Herald Tribune*, interviewed the Julianellis at Le Pavillon, dedicating an 'Inside Fashion' column to one of their open evening sandals: 'Born slowly,' she wrote, 'a new shoe is brilliant when it arrives and, likely as not, sways shoe history, since the Julianelli output is now factory-reproduced and reaches women from coast to coast.'

Now the Julianellis had two very powerful allies, Eleanor Lambert and Eugenia Sheppard.

When her daughter was about to enter kindergarten, Mabel knew that she wanted her to attend The Brearley School in New York. She wished to give her daughter an outstanding education, dancing school, piano lessons and a good orthodontist.

Mabel was working on references from Eleanor Lambert and Eugenia Sheppherd when a request for a parents' interview by the principal of the school came up, and without hesitation, she sent Charles.

Every woman found him charming, and this was a school run by women.

A tweedy assistant ushered him into a small office. "My wife and I would like very much for our daughter to attend The Brearley School," Charles said, self-conscious about his loose grammar in the taut atmosphere of the front lobby.

The Scottish principal, Jean Fair Mitchell, clad in her Assembly Hall black robe, raised one eyebrow when she saw him walk into her office. An electric shock flew from his hand to Miss Mitchell's when Charles crossed the overly thick rug to meet her. Anyone else would have melted in terror, but not Charles. The talk went to shoes and the well-informed Miss Mitchell said she admired the Lilt construction, but that flats were all she could wear. Graciously, Charles suggested a low heel style which he would personally make for her.

Mabel admitted to Cousin Anne that the pace of the business was uncontrollable, vying disastrously with her attempt to raise her daughter. She had to retain a baby nurse. In the end the baby nurse stayed for ten years; Jean McGowan was a sweet, nurturing woman, who typically brought mother and child home from the hospital and left, but this time Miss McGowan looked after Mabel's child for much longer. Jane remained friends with Miss McGowan until the lovely Scottish lady died in the 1970s.

Opposite: Charles created this shoe originally for The Brearley School's headmistress, Jean Fair Mitchell, to make her height as lofty as her presence in a low-heel shoe, 1951. Tassel suede loafer, this shoe 1970, heel, 1¼ inch. Photograph by John Manno.

Diana Vreeland drooled

At the start of 1950, in their apartment on East End Avenue, the Julianellis threw a series of vivacious parties to show off the first of Mabel's top-notch English antiques and French plates from Roslyn Rosier's shop on Fifty-Seventh Street. Roslyn was known for her daring Fifty-Seventh Street storefronts; one had Louis XV chairs standing in beach sand, which she had transported from East Hampton, Long Island in her Mercedes.

The Julianelli fêtes had the bubbly flavor of creativity and money, and the sophistication of good breeding – this time the blue bloods were Jewish. Everyone else, of diverse faiths, whether established or fledgling in their field, designers and fine artists alike – were there too, all mixed up with the contentious relatives.

The editors Kay Hayes and Diana Vreeland drooled over who was going to be the exclusive wearer of Charles' latest design – a silk pump with an oversized grosgrain bow and rhinestone circle ornament – and they growled at each other in their big-girl voices. Vivian Infantino, a young assistant editor at *Footwear News* came with her Italian dictionary and tossed Italian words at Charles. From *Harper's Bazaar* came Carmel Snow, in thick veiling with Alexey Brodovitch, who demonstrated the correct way to eat Caspian Sea caviar. Artist David Porter and his wife Marion talked about the abstract artists who were gathered on the eastern end of Long Island.

I. Miller's David Evins, Neapolitan shoe designer, Mario Valentino, and Palter and Deliso, swore off shoe talk for stuffing their mouths with caviar, while Bonwit Teller's legendary shoe aficionado Leon Turo, his sister, the posture-perfect Florence Eisner with her husband Bob, chatted in Southern accents with the witty Eugenia Sheppard, the lovely Mabel Schirmer (once married to Robert Schirmer of Schirmer Music Company) and designer Nettie Rosenstein and her sister-in-law, designer Eva Rosencrans. Ben Reig, antique dealer Roslyn Rosier and Dr Rosier swapped yard sale stories with the soignée Dorothy Shaver, president of Lord & Taylor. Alexander Lieberman, *Vogue's* art director, was invited with his wife Tatiana, and of course, Eleanor Lambert, and there was the exceptional pop in by a heavily powdered Helena Rubinstein, and Mr John or Norman Norell.

The guests munched on canapés from the Waldorf Astoria, fruit from Eisner & Co., and wines from Sherry Lehmann's Park Avenue store.

It was grand except for the usual post-party hullabaloo when the guests were gone. Papa Winkel would inevitably sit down hard in Mabel's armchair, splintering something, and Charles' sister Annette would complain that Helena Rubinstein stepped on her toe.

By now, Charles was so used to conformity and sacrifice in the name of family and country that it was second nature to him. He had resolved not to tell Mabel that he longed for a change, and that he was tired of using his head in the service of their ambition. She was the designer. He was a painter. It had been that way through the years while the events of their lives fueled and guided them in the direction of shoe design, and while his creativity ceased to be active to its own advantage.

Then news would come that would change everything.

In the summer of 1950, before the Long Island Expressway came east past Shirley, the Julianellis heard from artist David Porter about an old clapboard house for sale in East Hampton, Long Island, within walking distance of the Atlantic Ocean, and a mile from the neighboring Porters' ramshackle weekend retreat. Charles became unflinching about purchasing it, and two painters living in it without heating, lighting or plumbing, gave it up for a few hundred dollars.

In Porter's absence, the key was left with Roger Wilcox in Amagansett, so on their first visit the Julianellis had access only to the outside. The house hardly stood straight and the clapboards hung like splinters in some places, but it had survived the great hurricane of '38 – Porter had put that in his sales pitch. The Julianellis noticed it was on a tract of brush, ivy, thorny vines, stinging nettles, and withered wild roses that had tangled themselves around the foundation. "It's the boondocks!" screamed the metropolitan Mabel.

However, Charles saw solid features in the house – its sturdy saltbox frame and its two undamaged chimneys. It was surrounded by acres of wild cherry, scrub oak trees, aboriginal pines and lush forest cover, and was a green and verdant companion to the sea. Charles named the house Rose Cottage, and always referred to it that way.

Charles drove in his Chrysler to get the key from Wilcox after dropping Mabel and Janie at the haute-Victorian boarding house, the Hedges Inn, in East Hampton, where Route 27 turned east.

"Thank God for Henri Soulé," Mabel exclaimed upon learning that the Inn was the country branch of the superlative Le Pavillon in the City. Mabel was agonizingly shy around new people without shoe talk. And she'd find flaws in new people, such as their instant dismissal of her because she was short and their immediate attraction to her husband. It was better that she stayed put with her daughter in

Charles and Mabel in East Hampton, 1950. Mabel and Charles
found enormous acceptance, at that early time, among the
artists of East Hampton, for being artists themselves.

the lovely patio dining area, eating melon balls with spooned raspberry sauce. Of course, she had no idea at the time who these Wilcox people were.

From his first encounter with painters Roger Wilcox and his wife, Lucia, Charles' whetted appetite for painting could stand no further delay, and rounding up paints and brushes and canvas was priority when he got back to the City.

It was a few days after Memorial Day Weekend, a time in the year which the East Hampton residents called the start of the Season. Charles' polished black shoes sent the dust flying when he stepped down from the Chrysler, and the edges of his pant cuffs were instantly coated with potato dust from the fields in East Hampton, which sifted in monotone through the sand of the Atlantic. The ebb and flow of the wind, recently traversing the ocean, crossing over the Amagansett shore, over the railroad tracks, was soothing, as were hawks sounds and other birds that Charles could not name. He went to the Wilcox place happily alone.

Scrawny, tall, laid-back Roger Wilcox was a painter and a carpenter. At times Roger and his wife, Lucia, who was a painter born in Italy, showed their work in their high hollow barn, or work of other artists they had coaxed into their pool of creativity, forming a colony of painters, such as Willem de Kooning, Elaine de Kooning, Lee Krasner, Jackson Pollock, and painter/sculptor Max Ernst, and muscians, for example flamenco guitarist, Carlos Montoya, who frolicked, barbequed and drank together. Wilcox's renovated barn contained rough-timbered walls, suitable for hanging his wife's tall oil paintings – triumphantly rising apparitions vividly colored or shrouded in white and grey.

Some thought the sea gave the place an artist's light, for which the East End was known. Visitors thought it was the salt air that made the barn smell briny, not knowing that often barns like that were built in the two-hundred year-old tradition of using seaweed for insulation.

At the end of the dirt road, the grass was dotted with artists standing at easels, pottery wheels, and sculpture. "We sometimes like to work shoulder to shoulder," Wilcox told Charles. The place appeared to be full of things desired and forbidden. Cadmium and chartreuse oil paints separated in the sun. Hardened paint stained fingernails. The landscape painters gazed at the barn. Other painters

"The end of the 1940s and the 1950s when Mabel was bursting on the fashion scene were very exciting times; the writers were E. E. Cummings, Djuna Barnes. It was a different time of life. It was very productive in art. In theater there was Tennessee Williams, William Inge, Arthur Miller. There was so much that came out of that time; it was an extraordinary time for creativity. Think about the 1950s in East Hampton; think about the artists and those artists were very famous, Jackson Pollock, Willem de Kooning, and all the writers coming out to Long Island. It was a very freeing period for artists. And Mabel was involved too, during that early time, in fashion and all that related to it."

Gerald Blum, actor, innovator of fashion trends, former Executive Vice President of Lord & Taylor.

splattered their canvases with random color. Charles learned that this kind of painting was called abstract. He saw art first in Onorata's illustrated writings of the Saints.

Charles had looked at the Italian masters, while he attended functions at the Metropolitan Museum of Art in New York – once in 1942 for the donation of Julianelli shoes by Saks Fifth Avenue to the Costume Institute, and again at the beginning of 1950 for the 'Adam in the Looking Glass' exhibit, which featured a men's shoe by Julianelli.

On each occasion Charles had slipped away from the reception to visit the painting galleries on the second floor to see Raffaello, Botticelli and Ghirlandaio – Italian masters whose names rolled off the tongue, just like his own. It was nice to know they were there, on Fifth Avenue. But Charles had never seen painting the way it was done at the Wilcox place.

Wilcox led Charles a few feet to the wood's edge, past parts of a rusted hayfork. "I'm trying to do something with the hayfork, the way Ernst might do, just for fun," he chuckled.

"Quite a collection," observed Charles, "I mean the artists."

"We can talk up here," said Wilcox, "Cooler up here."

"Hot today, for May," said Charles.

The two men leaned against a tree, staring out the way people do after weather-related talk.

"Yes, my collection," said Wilcox amused. "It's a funny thing, but I am more gratified by their talent than I am by my own."

"No one would say that in my world," said Charles.

"You see, Charles, here it's not a question of competition, but love for the art, everyone's art."

Charles saw a woman near the barn, stooping to take something from the grass, as Wilcox was saying, "She's collecting stones for her new painting." Charles was instantly fascinated by the woman, the black waves of her hair curling over her basket.

BY MABEL JULIANELLI

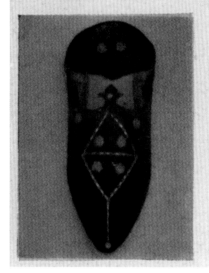

Mrs. Julianelli: "A major change in men's shoes . . . light in weight and more pliable." Opposite page: soft toe, dark brown calfskin cut low, unlined. Left: Moroccan shoe, stamped gold design.

Above: Mabel Julianelli's quote about men's footwear in *Vogue*, 1950. Caption for photo by Herbert Matter/Condé Nast Archive; Copyright © Condé Nast Publications.

Opposite: 'Clothes and the Man': Julianelli men's shoe, *Vogue*, 1950. Herbert Matter/Condé Nast Archive; Copyright © Condé Nast Publications.

"That's Lucia, my wife," said Wilcox. "Well, here's your key then," he added.

Arriving back at the Hedges Inn Charles ran to find Mabel. "We should stay here –" he said when he found her in the room, dozing on the bed in Capri pants and a short-sleeved shirt. She bolted up with a huge smile on her face.

"– surrounded by artists – you'll love it, and Janie too," he was talking rapidly, "I want to live here. I want to go back to my painting."

"I'm sorry darling, but we can't live here," Mabel said, "because a while ago I called the office, and we've just won the Coty Award."

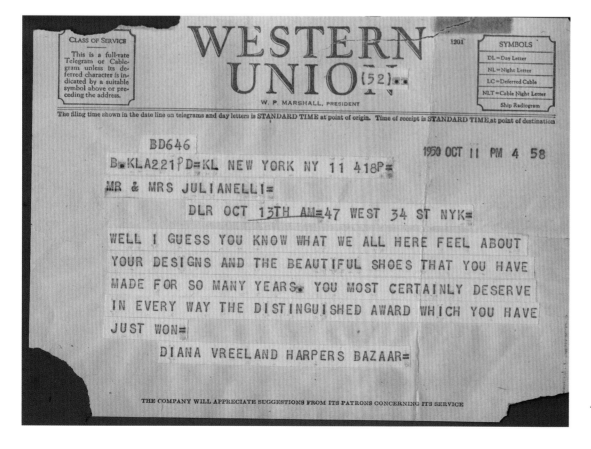

Left: Diana Vreeland, *Harper's Bazaar*. Taken from a Western Union telegram to Mr & Mrs Julianelli on October 13th, 1950, the day after the Coty Awards.
Opposite: "Laces for men are a nuisance," Mabel said. She took inspiration for her pin-point perforated flat from a men's shoe she designed for The Costume Institute's exhibit 'Adam in the Looking Glass'. Heel: 1 inch, 1950. Photograph by John Manno.

The bare low heels. Mrs Friedman wore a pair of these shoes the day Mabel and Iris and Steve Friedman met Gloria Swanson at Mme. Romaine de Lyon's omelet eatery in New York. Ms Swanson told Mabel that because she was petite too, she adored Mabel's stilettos and had read that Mabel only wore them. They were, Swanson attested, the ultimate in comfort. Heel: 1⅜ inches, 1970. Courtesy of Iris Friedman. Photograph by John Manno.

'Little bits of nothing'

"THEY'RE NAKED!" members of the audience sizzled, as six gorgeous models walked on stage in Julianelli shoes. Of course they were referring to the shoes – 'invisible sandals', one critic said – 'little bits of nothing' – 'most revolutionary shoe-ideas of the decade' – 'Mabel and Charles Julianelli's brainchildren!'

It was October 12th, 1950, the glamorous night of The American Fashion Critics' Awards, presented at the Waldorf Astoria Hotel in New York.

Florence Pritchett, fashion editor and playmate of a young House of Representatives member, John F. Kennedy, narrated the Fashion Parade to an audience of publishing moguls, including William Randolph Hearst, and fashion legends – among them, Norman Norell, Hattie Carnegie, Lilly Daché, Pauline Trigère and Omar Kiam, and the Mayor of New York, Vincent R. Impellitteri.

That evening, with the Grand Ballroom to frame her, a victorious Mabel Julianelli was portrayed by the *New York Herald Tribune* as a 'gently charming small brunette with enormous black eyes and a ready laugh.' *The New Yorker* said 'she looked as though she were made of ribbon candy.'

Two days before, an invitation, via Western Union telegram, from politician and New York City's greeter Grover A. Whalen invited the Julianellis to dine:

'Mrs. Whalen and I are giving a small dinner party in honor of the 1950 American Fashion Critics' Award Winners prior to the fashion show and presentation. We would be delighted to have you join us for dinner at 7:00 in the Janssen Suite, Waldorf Astoria Hotel, Black Tie, R.S.V.P., Grover A. Whalen'

The day of the event, Mabel was at her office, sitting grandly in a new white wicker fan-back chair, purchased from her friend, antique dealer Roslyn Rosier, from her Fifty-Seventh Street shop, now exploding with wicker. Mabel was thrilled by anything oversized when she was in the context of its framework. A backward glance at its high peacock fan and she felt blissfully taller.

Mabel was busy honing an acceptance speech on her Underwood typewriter: 'There's never been a better season for the consumer to say, Get to the point! For, at the moment, there is a serious battle raging on the shoe front and it's called, to point or not to point.'

She continued: 'Now my mother taught me never to point, except at the pastry tray, but for the past five years, I have been pointing shoes…' Mabel knew she was too afraid to give the speech, and would have to make Charles do it. She ripped out the sheet and rolled in a new one. 'Now *her* mother taught *her*…' It would be a knock-out speech with Charles delivering it.

Over at the Waldorf, members of the Arrangements Committee, Mrs William T. Gaynor, Mrs Anthony Drexel Duke, Mrs Henry Ford II and Mrs Alfred Gwynne Vanderbilt among them, made their presence known, officiating on the stage above what would be, that night, the largest and most brilliantly dressed audience ever to assemble under the Waldorf roof. The place cards were set with a rather uncivilized system by which those receiving their accolades would be gawked at from an embarrassingly close range by those already famous in fashion , commerce and politics.

At Table 1 would be the Hon. Grover A. Whalen, Chairman of the Board of Coty Inc. and his wife, and H.E. Brigadier General Carlos P. Romulo of the Philippines and Mrs Romulo; criminal attorney Lloyd Paul Stryker and his wife would sit at Table 2; newspaper publisher William Randolph Hearst at Table 3; industry leader Adam Gimbel at Table 4. Mabel and Charles Julianelli and guests would sit at Table 18. It did seem a bit hodge-podge, especially if you were not seasoned in the art of seating arrangement. Mabel loved the perspective at Table 18, a little removed, but all-seeing.

Eugenia Sheppard at *The New York Herald Tribune* was sharpening her informal chatter for the period during the supper dance, as was Anne Thatcher Fuller over at *Flair*. 'Mabel is a native New Yorker who can't remember the time she didn't have a pencil in her hand,' Ms Sheppard jotted down, 'having drawn pictures since she was two years old…'

At the same time, Mabel went on writing her speech – Charles's speech. To gain momentum she would begin with her Chopine platform sandal, exhibited in 1944 at the Museum of Modern Art. That would clearly set the tone. She'd mention her studies at Pratt Institute, Charles's time as First Lieutenant in the Army, Mabel and Charles working together for commercial manufacturers who produced thousands of shoes a day from their designs, and finally, getting their own design studio, where each shoe was hand-lasted.

She would tell the little story about when they were getting started, how the New York manufacturers would say to her: 'Go to Paris, Mabel – Set up there, and then we can promote you.' Yet, while she and Charles took many trips to Paris, they never opened their design studio in Paris because it was important for both of them to set up in New York. She would end by saying:

Portrait of Mabel and Charles in the American Fashion
Critics' Awards (Coty Awards) program, 1950.

'The reason a smart shop goes overboard to sponsor us today is perhaps because we forced them to look in America for new talent!'

Softening, she would show off the Julianellis as the husband and wife team about town, hob-knobbing at the Barberry Room in the Berkshire Hotel with Moss Hart and Raymond Massey. She would reminisce about their courtship on the Penny Bridge – not too far back – maybe that was too far. She didn't want the audience to know how young the two really were starting out.

The true strength of the speech was not simply its intelligence, but its vivacity – a fast-paced-exceed-the-speed-limit account of their rise. Charles had better take a nap. Its wittiness was important – how it would entertain and win the undivided attention of the jury of seventy fashion editors of magazines, syndicates and newspapers, with Eugenia Sheppard at the helm, who would read the citations of the jury.

An hour before, in the ballroom of the Waldorf, Lester Gaba was working on the staging for this fifteen-dollar per person fashion show and supper dance for the benefit of the Children's Unit of Memorial Hospital. Special curtains, lights and backgrounds were reminiscent of Broadway. William Richardson was adjusting the lighting, Stanley Melba annotated the music and Frank Stevens worked on the *mise-en-scène*.

Charles sat tensely in a green silk armchair in the Park Avenue lobby, smoking a cigarette, looking a lot like Cary Grant and Gregory Peck – all dolled up thanks to Mabel in a *tux* so tight there was even a hint of Liberace.

Charles thought of their house in East Hampton, the land around it, the small carriage house to the west, its outhouse detached, with *his* and *her* toilet holes carved out of a wooden board. Toilet holes – thinking of them at the Waldorf seemed ridiculous. He hadn't yet walked to the ocean. He hadn't yet seen the carriage house, but he would. He would force Mabel to come with him, and if he couldn't, he would try to bribe her with sweets from Schrafft's.

At the Coty Awards the Waldorf's ballroom was packed. After the National Anthem the first course was bisque. Charles wore a navy suit and a dark blue silk tie. Mabel herself was a perfect masterpiece in a black Traina-Norell cocktail dress, accessorized by a flapper-inspired crystal bead necklace, set with onyx and citrine, once worn by her mother, which she tied in a knot at her bosom. But despite the flawlessness of their appearance, Mabel was nervous, so nervous that she inadvertently tugged too hard on the knot and the necklace broke, bouncing beads off her bosom and into the bisque of

Right: The Thread Sandal, 1950.

The Julianelli Naked Evening Sandal
Opposite: The Circe, the most celebrated 'naked' evening sandal of 1950, won the Coty Award.
This page: The Circe naked sandal; Mabel always wore it with a Norman Norell. This variation has an ankle strap on a raised back, heel: 4 inches, 1950.
Photograph by John Manno.

The Julianelli Naked Evening Sandal
This page: Stripping sandal with delicately gathered, hand-cut threads of leather, V-strapped around the ankle, heel: 3 inches, 1960. Photograph by John Manno.
Opposite: Threads of purple strips, self-lined dancing sandal. This naked sandal style took off when Sophia Loren posed in it in gold for US *Harper's Bazaar*, December, 1982. Heel: 3½ inches. Photograph by John Manno.

The Julianelli Naked Evening Sandal

The Julianelli Naked Evening Sandal
This page: The naked look, suggestive of the Circe naked sandal from the 1950s, this version with a halter back and V-strap, burgundy strippy sandal, heel: 3½ inches, 1980. Photograph by John Manno. *Opposite:* Pastel thread sandal, also known as the 'Barefoot'. Infinitesimal stripping of leather, heel, 3½ inches, 1980. Photograph by John Manno.

more than one dinner guest. The table was virtually in the air with guests under it looking for the beads, while Mabel was spellbound with mortification, although in disbelief she noticed that nobody beyond her table took notice. When the party had collected itself, Charles was at her side defending her with his particularly becoming style of gallantry, "Mabel's been trying to find a way to get me to buy her pearls."

The other Coty Award winners that evening were designers Charles James and Bonnie Cashin, who received a Winnie (the bronze figure by Malina Hoffman), Nancy Melcher, designer of nylon lingerie for Vanity Fair Mills, and the Julianellis, who received a Special Award, a silver plaque.

Eleanor Lambert's accolades in her press release and the Awards program were reported in newspapers and on radio and television the next day:

> *'The Julianellis, a young shoe designing team, were cited for their high standards of artistry and craftsmanship which reflect their creative talent, and because in their sponsorship of the naked look in shoes which actually contains the foot securely, they have had an impressive influence on shoe fashion throughout the world.'*

Julianelli shoes were worn with the winning dresses of premier American designer Charles James, to whom meticulous construction was critical. James wrote to the Julianellis on October 14th following a fashion show which was aired on NBC television: 'I thought a word of appreciation due to you for lending me your shoes to use with my dresses. I only had the opportunity to look at them closely today in the television show, and I was struck by the beauty of their design, and above all, by the wonderful proportion of the detail.'

Of course, it was the construction. Every Julianelli shoe's paramount *raison d'être*, its beginning and its end, was its construction. Most applauds went to the Circe style and two other styles representing the 'naked look'. The Julianellis never told anyone how the shoe stayed on the foot – telegrams and letters all asked the same thing: 'how did you do it?' Was it Mabel's design, or Charles'? Everyone showed genuine amazement – *Harpers Bazaar*'s Carmel Snow and Diana Vreeland, *Vogue*'s Jessica Daves, *Women's Wear Daily*, the regional stores, the New York City department stores, the suppliers like Allied Kid Company and Burlington Mills.

One editor, Virginia Chumley from the Chattanooga *News Free Press*, wrote: 'Now on this latter award I agree thoroughly because when anybody can make nothing out of something and make it

699 Madison Avenue Regent 7-6611

New York

Charles James

Dear Mr. and Mrs. Julianelli,

I thought a word of appreciation due to you for lending me your shoes to use with my dresses. I only had the opportunity to look at them closely today in the television show, and I was struck by the beauty of their design, and above all, by the wonderful proportion of the detail!

Yours sincerely,

Charles James

CHARLES JAMES

CJ:p
Dict. but
not read

Mr. and Mrs. Charles Julianelli
c/o Lord & Taylor
New York, New York

October 14, 1950

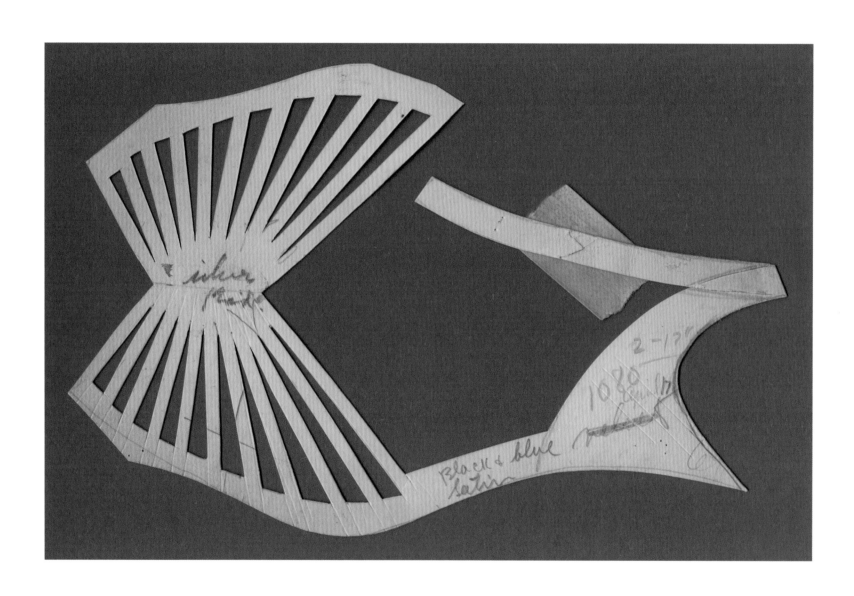

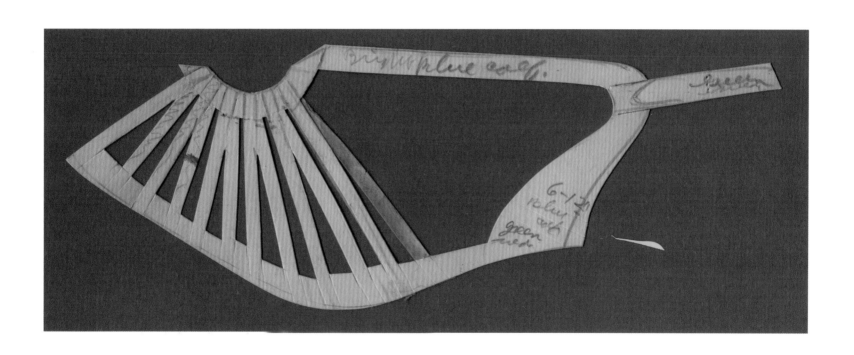

Opposite: Charles Julianelli for Julianelli Inc. Pattern for blue
and black satin strippy evening sandal (front), 1956.
Above: Charles Julianelli for Julianelli Inc. Pattern for blue
and black satin strippy evening sandal (side), 1956.

actually stay on the foot—and most amazing of all, succeed in having it called a *shoe*—they have really done something!'

The Julianellis had been in partnership for nearly twenty years, entering into marriage twelve years after they met at the pattern factory, and then, only after they believed they could handle people's criticism under Charles' thick coat of confidence. After that night, New York City exploded beneath their feet – they were the inventors of a magical shoe, not seen before, not worn before. Its origins were the Julianelli innovations of the 1940s. A 'first' was not a light bulb going off in one's head – it was an enterprise of effort, thought and observation.

A press member wrote, 'Perhaps no other young designers than the Julianellis ever had so many firsts in such short a time, and certainly not a husband and wife designing team.'

All the Julianellis heard was their name.

"I love our name," said Mabel, "even if there is no letter 'J' in the Italian alphabet!"

"I'm glad, May," said Charles.

"Finally, I belong to it and it belongs to me."

"For as long as you want it to," said Charles.

Through the 1950s, all activity quickened, nearly driving them mad. Success for the Julianellis sometimes had to be recast to make room for their daughter, but more often their daughter was recast to make room for their success.

The Circe, the original bare sandal which won the Coty Award and was worn in the Fashion Parade at the Coty Award ceremony, expanded into a group of shoes with very high heels, yet with inexplicable comfort. Mabel and Charles exaggerated the Circe's delicacy with extra windings of finer strips, which had all the podiatrists in New York scratching their heads. The term 'leather stripping' became synonymous with Julianelli.

The Circe showed up at a patio party at The Cloisters in the pages of *Town & Country*, at the Stork Club paired with a Hattie Carnegie black silk taffeta coat in *The New York Times*' Fashion of the Times, and dancing in a lounge in *Life Magazine*, paired with Traina-Norell and Omar Kiam.

Opposite left: Mabel Julianelli for Julianelli Inc. Sketch of her evening ankle-strap slipper, showing how she mixed in one shoe, hues of color and fabrications, kid skin and suede, 1950. © 2010 Jane Julianelli.
Opposite right top: Saks Fifth Avenue Ad including a sketch of Mabel and Charles, 1950. Saks Fifth Avenue.
Opposite right bottom: Windowpane version of naked sandal, 1951.

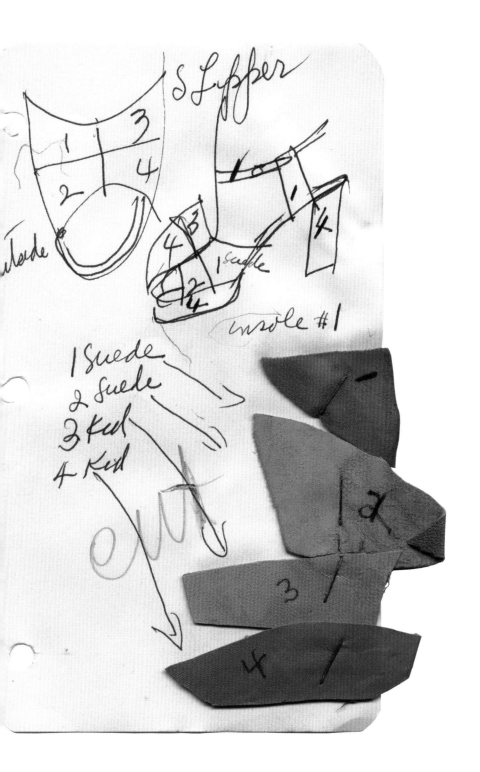

Rose Cottage

When the Julianellis walked into Rose Cottage for the first time, the beams and joists vibrated and nails in the pine planks popped. The plaster hung from the ceiling like paper doilies. With no electricity and few windows, it was as dark as midnight. Paintings on torn canvas were left tacked to the walls by sellers who happily fled with their new-found money. It seemed dismal and in terrible disrepair, but Charles wanted to live there. It breathed oil paint. He thought of the painters at the Wilcox place, and Lucia.

After buying the house on seven acres, with an another fourteen acres to the east, Charles drew plans for a renovation on several pieces of cardboard, and in October, 1950, two weeks after the Coty Awards ceremony, blueprints were filed by the architect, Leonard C. Henry, stamped by the surveyor, Walter E. Brady of Southampton and approved by the East Hampton Town Building Department.

During the renovation, Mabel was on a Coty cloud and desperate to get back to the City, having had enough country when she was growing up in Brooklyn; Charles, however, longed to return to the Wilcox place. He made a handsome figure on the job site. He was always formal, even here, in polished black shoes, khaki trousers, a black leather jacket over a shirt and tie. Mabel took a picture of him straddling a corner of the addition.

As she stared through the lens of her Brownie Instamatic she was startled by a sad look in his eyes. A faraway longing was one thing – she had a faraway longing too, in the direction of New York – but his was something else. First of all he looked fatigued, but with the punishing years of work catching up with him, what could one expect? There was something emancipating in the look too, as if he anticipated a welcomed change. Her attention remained concentrated on him while she remembered the time he left the Penn Station platform to go into the Army, and how she tried to talk herself out of the fear that he would never be the same again.

Lucia Wilcox flung bird seed as she walked with Charles along Abrahams Path, across the railroad track, left on Route 27, right along Indian Wells, and south to the ocean.

Italian, small, with sharp features, olive skin, Lucia blazed in an orange cotton sarong fitted tight across her body, barely held by a turquoise scorpion pin. She jingled with red and green enamel bangles that swallowed both arms up to the elbows. Charles could smell sweet Basil on her.

Charles and Janie, East Hampton, 1954.

Lucia looked up at him. "You are our first fashion designer here, but," she shrugged,

"I accept you and respect your talent, just like Pollock, or de Kooning or anyone else."

"Did you read about us in the paper?" he asked, somewhat embarrassed, but flattered.

"Yes, but I knew – even before – that you are a very fine artist," she said.

"Mabel is too," Charles said.

"I'm sure," said Lucia, "but your Mabel does not seem to want to visit us."

"Mabel is very shy except with fashion people," he said without any defensiveness.

"Well then, we'll have to cultivate some fashion people here to please her," Lucia said smiling, without taking her eyes off him.

Lucia told Charles about the Long Island farms at the turn of the century, the rows which the tractors made running down to the sand,and how it was said that salt water irrigated the potato crops.

"Of course," she laughed, "that is a story told by the same *spiritisti* who also spoke of the crops growing in the ocean, and the farmers riding the waves on their tractors. I believe, do you?"

Of course he believed in the *spiritisti*, Italy's spiritual thinkers.

Somehow the Julianellis made time for family life gatherings in their New York apartment at 33 East End Avenue during the Christmas holidays. They enjoyed a sumptuous Christmas dinner prepared by their German cook, Dora. Charles would say at the end of the meal, "Mabel, you did a fine job," and everyone would chuckle because they knew she hadn't touched a ladle, but that was just his gallant way. The cousins, Janie, Ona and Johnny performed skits; it was the best gift they could give Charles. Mabel, despite her Papa, loved Christmas because Charles loved Christmas and loved it in New York.

When the Julianellis moved up the block to 130 East End Avenue, with a view of the East River, obstructed slightly by the trees of Carl Schultz Park, the cousins dropped water balloons on the doormen. Johnny looked like a young Elvis Presley; Ona was a blond angel, and Janie was the mischief of the three.

Other good times were spent in East Hampton; half dead from the office, the Julianellis would trudge through rituals relating to weekenders from New York City; storm windows went up, storm windows went down; pipes were bled. Trapped squirrels were escorted out. They shopped at the farm stands

Mabel tries to sketch at the beach, 1956.

Mabel and Charles at Rose Cottage, 1954.

along Montauk Highway, and Mabel started to bake – strawberry shortcake, baked Alaska and popovers in her Garland stove. Charles sat in the sun, in the backyard, on railroad ties that stepped up to a grassy terrace, and painted, while Mabel drew with charcoals. Charles liked to watch the paint separate in the heat. Sometimes it took hours.

When Charles wasn't feeding the ducks at the Nature Trail on David's Lane with Janie or teaching her how to swim at Barnes Landing, he went off to see property for sale and once came home with five acres of land off Bridge Lane on Sagaponack Pond in Bridgehampton, another time, two acres with a dilapidated mansion and carriage house off Terbell Lane on Hook Pond, East Hampton, with more purchases on the way. He chose pond front, he told Mabel, "just to be romantic", so that they could build a little dock and he would take her out in a rowboat.

Some Saturday nights Mabel wore a Tom Brigance beach pajama with several abundant yards of chantung floating behind her, her straw mules, her hair colored with blue crepe paper streamers, as she hosted a garden party for her New York chums and Charles' artist friends on the terrace bordered by Charles' zinnia and dahlia beds, parties where

the artists talked about fashion and the fashion people talked about art.

Each year arrived and passed with almost unblemished domestic euphoria. There was that little business of Charles' visits to Lucia. Mabel never said a word and tried to loosen up a bit at the Wilcox place, since it was what summer afternoons called for. Charles painted there or rocked with Roger on ladder backs against a shaded wall, smelling spices from his native Italy on top of the greasy aroma of oil paint. Janie had a painting lesson with Lucia, and one or two small landscapes depicting Rose Cottage were sold at East Hampton's Guild Hall Clothesline art show, with Lucia's finishing touch on each – small white flicks of her brush, capping a tree or a cloud. Mabel saw with apprehension that Charles, who had been unsettled for such a long time, was lifted by the possibility that life could go his way. But what way was that, she wondered?

Bread and eggs – got to pick some up – remembered Charles. Driving over the broad central road of East Hampton, on which hoof prints of cows herded to Montauk had long been paved over. Charles passed the Edward's Movie Theater, Chez Labot, and stopped at Bohack, where fresh baked bread was thirteen cents a loaf, and eggs twenty-three cents a dozen. He hummed a Cole Porter song, *From This Moment On*, and thought he'd tell Mabel he loved her when he got back and call her by her nickname, May.

Charles could not help wishing that Mabel had the same love for the place. Slowly Rose Cottage grew on Mabel when her friends started buying houses – Roslyn Rosier decorated her East Hampton house in all white and was one of the first to do it. Her house overlooked Georgica Cove, and was across West End Road from the infamous Beales' Grey Gardens house.

Mabel got to know the neighbors, whose children played with Janie. When children's author, Mariana Foster, needed a little girl to pose for a *Life* magazine spread about the heroine of her books, Miss Flora McFlimsey, Janie posed in Foster's studio behind the local inn and across from the beach road. It was from the porch of that inn fifty years before that gossip columnists for the local gazette spied on who went with whom to the beach.

Even the 'naked look' for evening, winner of the Coty Award, became more naked when Mabel took up sketching on the beach a few blocks from Rose Cottage. It was a wild stretch of dunes and shore, with nothing on it – no lifeguard or cabanas, or colored flags to tell you how rough the ocean was, as on the East Hampton Main Beach where Janie and her friends played.

Mabel arrived in pedal pushers, an oversized white shirt and glasses, with pad and pencil. She sketched there whether she was accompanied by Charles, Janie, or the whole family; the Azzaritis came from Ohio and the Leydens came from Silver Springs, Maryland. Mama Onorata came from the family home in Fairview, always for Mabel, so full of spaghetti and inspiration.

"I don't want us to be remembered for comfort, or proportion, or for containing the foot securely, or for designing a work of art – not any of that," Mabel told her sister-in-law Annette, sitting beside her on a blanket in the sand. "I want us to be remembered for sex appeal, what I used to call *girl appeal*. Isn't that what every woman wants?" Annette made the sign of the cross.

When asked how she invented the 'naked look', whatever she replied at the time, Mabel would always think to herself, her inspiration came from the beach. She had experienced her feet in a new way, slipping easily through the sand, and she wanted to duplicate that released feeling in a shoe.

Above: Mabel at the beach, 1960.
Opposite: Mabel Julianelli for Julianelli Inc.
Sketch of Little Tie Oxford with swatches, 1960.
© 2010 Jane Julianelli.

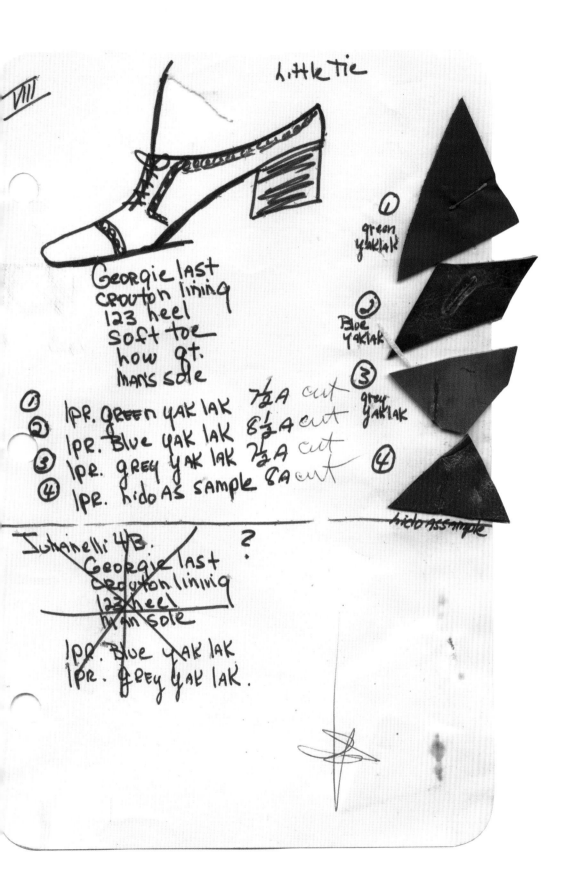

little tie

VIII

Georgie last
Crouton lining
123 heel
Soft toe
how gt.
mans sole

① green yaklak
② Blue yaklak
③ grey yaklak
④ hido as sample

① 1PR. GREEN YAK lak 7½A cut
② 1PR. Blue yak lak 8½A cut
③ 1PR. grey yak lak 7½A cut
④ 1PR. hido as sample 8A cut

hido as sample

Juhanelli 4B: ?
Georgie last
Crouton lining
123 heel
man sole

1PR. Blue yak lak
1PR. grey yak lak.

Opposite: Asymmetrical soft-band mule red,
seen on the Côte d'Azur, heel: 3⅝ inches, 1960.
Photograph by John Manno.
Left: Mabel Julianelli for Julianelli Inc.
Sketch of t-strap (side) with swatches, 1960.
© 2010 Jane Julianelli.

Life outside Rose Cottage

During the late 50s through the early 60s, Charles could not easily leave Rose Cottage. These were the years his happiness was greatest, but Mabel and Eleanor Lambert out-voted him. Charles and Mabel moved around the globe both together and separately. When Charles traveled without her, especially to Paris, Mabel was constantly agitated. For one thing he smoked too much in Europe, those little dark cigarettes, and for another, who knew whose eyes were on him? Chanel had glanced at him once on the Rue Cambon, once on the Rue du Faubourg Saint-Honoré. There was that incident with Cole Porter regarding a French-cut chicken at Café de Flore on the Boulevard Saint-Germain. However, Charles always came home to Mabel and the place where he could relax and listen to his recordings of the Don Shirley Trio and the Dave Brubeck Quartet.

The fashion business of yesterday thrived on pleasantry and etiquette. Gifts prevailed, and the citadel of gift giving, New York City, provided legions of sentimental considerations. In a small powder-blue address book Mabel kept the names of important people who were responsible for her success; beyond that she kept in her head their favorite indulgences and passions – Jessica Daves, editor-in-chief of *Vogue*, Carmel Snow, editor-in-chief of *Harper's Bazaar*, and fashion editor, Diana Vreeland all received flowers from Irene Hayes Wadley & Smythe. Dorothy Shaver, president of Lord & Taylor, received a Scope cigarette holder. For Kay Hayes, accessories editor at *Vogue*, Mabel selected a diamond-shaped Cartier silk scarf.

Mabel received impassioned thank you notes: 'It's impossible to really tell you how sentimental I am about you and about everything you've ever given me,' said one, '…you are both so dear to me and I love you so much … my love and affection to both of you.'

One 1961 note from a favorite client in Missouri, Bettie Rice, who had visited them on a recent buying trip, scared Mabel quite a bit:

'…thank you again dear for the lovely candy. Was so sorry to see that Charles has been feeling so bad. What's wrong? It doesn't make sense for all of us to be in this 'rat race' – I, for one, am slowing down and trying to make my guy do the same.'

Had somebody finally guessed that Charles was not well?

At the beginning of March, 1962, while Mabel was in Spain, on one of the business trips without him, Charles was exceedingly weak, and this made his enthusiasm to pack the car and take Janie out to East Hampton for the weekend appear strained. On Friday he picked her up at the New York Society Library, after shoving into the trunk a particularly heavy rug from the apartment. He endured an unusual shortness of breath, but they headed off anyway.

Over the weekend, he had chest pains and nausea. The following Monday, Charles had a heart attack and was admitted to the Wickersham Hospital on Lexington Avenue, and immediately put in an oxygen tent.

"Don't leave me, my love," whispered Mabel, small and alone in a hotel room somewhere in Madrid, grasping the Western Union telegram to her heart. Her words startled her, but not nearly as much as the ringing in the phone pressed tightly to her ear, the impersonal noise of transcontinental failure, intensified by an operator's voice repeating that all lines were busy.

Mabel sat in a smart black and white Donald Brook's suit, her Koret clutch bag and her gloves on the bed where she had placed them. Suddenly she threw them across the room. She wondered how she could bring back all the years, love the man more and the shoe business less, because at that moment a kind-hearted man was taking his last breath and she was too late and too far from him to do anything about it.

Mabel and Charles, 1960.

S.F.A's heel-lights

When it's a season of intriguing back-interest—glitter follows. In S.F.A.'s exclusive new collection of evening sandals, the slender heels are a-blaze with closely set rhinestones. Left to right—CONFETTI HEEL, cross strap, dyeable white satin with multicolored stones, 39.95. TWINKLING T-STRAP in rhinestone-set silver kid, 49.95. FIRELIT HALTER, dyeable white satin with rhinestones, 37.95. Shoe Collections, Fourth Floor.

glitter bag by Koret

—superb little purse that sparkles in hand. Rhinestone leaves on black, or brown satin, 55.00—or Koret black velvet, 55.00. All pl... Handbag Collections, Street SWEPT-BACK SHEATH, of the started the new heel interest at 250.00 in our Evening

SAKS FIFTH AVENUE

...th Avenue advertisements on Pages 31, 54, 107, 110, 112, 121, 127, 130 and 133   at Rockefeller Center a...

192

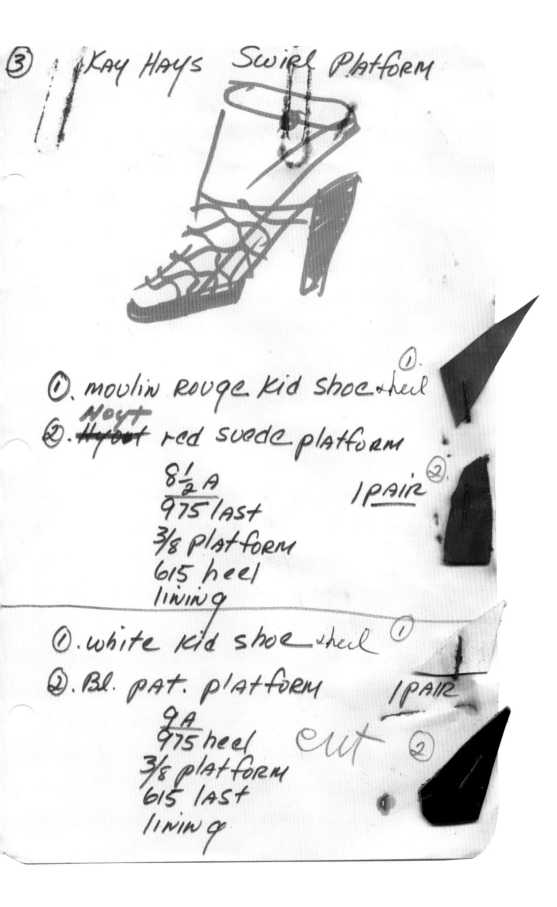

③ | KAY HAYS   Swirl Platform

①. moulin rouge. kid shoe & heel

②. ~~Noyt~~ red suede platform

8½ A
975 last
3/8 platform
615 heel
lining

1 PAIR ②

①. white kid shoe & heel ①

②. Bl. pat. platform   1 PAIR

9 A
975 heel
3/8 platform   cut   ②
615 last
lining

Opposite: Saks Fifth Avenue's heel-lights,
rhinestone-set heel back interest, 1955.
Saks Fifth Avenue.
This page: Mabel Julianelli for Julianelli Inc.
Sketch of her Swirl platform, an exclusive
for *Vogue* Accessories Editor, Kay Hays,
with leather swatches attached, 1959.
© 2010 Jane Julianelli.

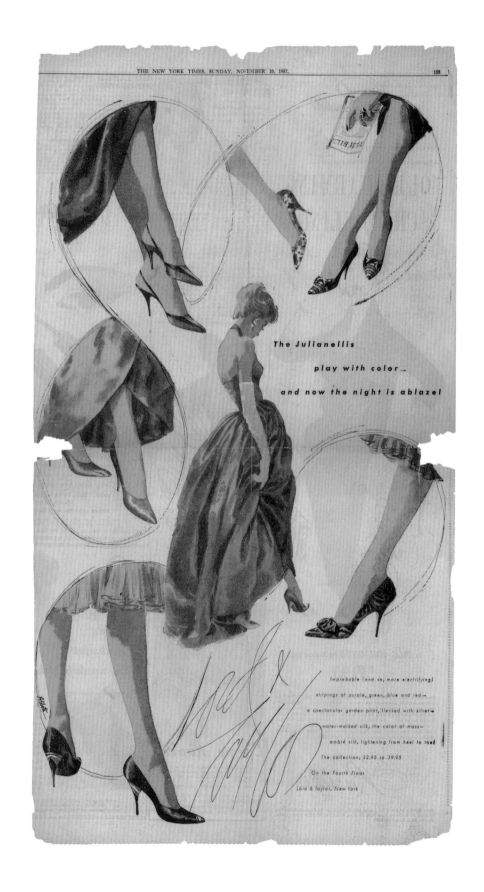

The Julianellis

play with color —

and now the night is ablaze!

Improbable (and so, more electrifying)

stripings of purple, green, blue and red —

a spectacular garden print, flecked with silver —

water-marked silk, the color of moss —

ombré silk, lightening from heel to toe!

The collection, 32.95 to 39.95

On the Fourth Floor

Lord & Taylor, New York

194

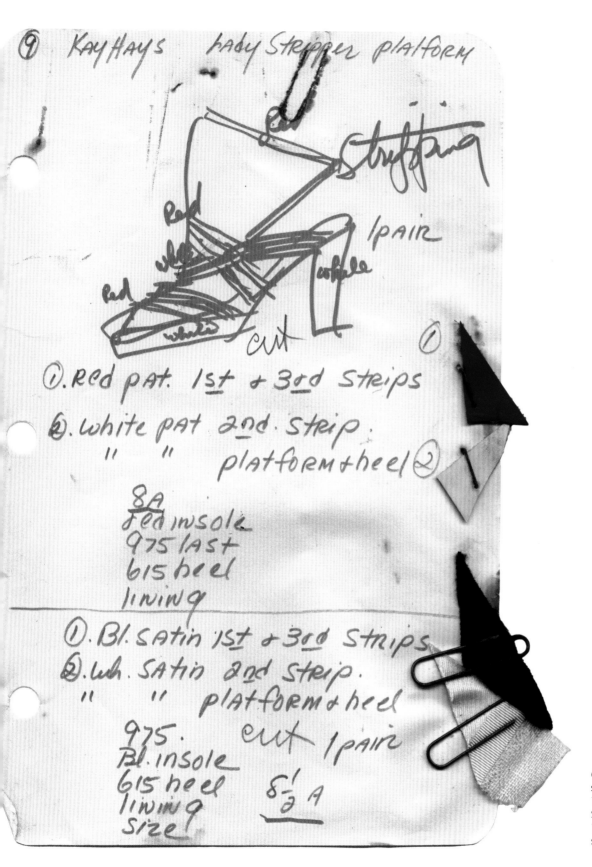

⑨ Kay Hays   Lady Stripper platform

stripping

Red

white

1 pair

white

cut

①. Red pat. 1st & 3rd strips

②. white pat 2nd. strip.
    "   "   platform & heel ②

8A
Red insole
975 last
615 heel
lining

①. Bl. satin 1st & 3rd strips
②. wh. satin 2nd. strip.
    "   "   platform & heel
975.   cut 1 pair
Bl. insole
615 heel   8½ A
lining
size 9

Opposite: The Color Collection: pumps and strippings for Lord & Taylor, 1957. Lord & Taylor. *This page:* Mabel Julianelli for Julianelli Inc. Sketch of Lady Stripper platform, an exclusive for *Vogue* Accessories Editor, Kay Hays, with leather swatches attached, 1960. © 2010 Jane Julianelli.

Mabel and Charles in the 86th Street apartment, 1961.

Part Two
Mabel Without Charles

Opposite: Tracery of delicate confetti strips twisted on the vamp and at the halter, ankle-tied, 1980. Mrs Friedman wore this evening sandal when dancing the Pasa Doble in Madrid with Mr Friedman. Heel: 3½ inches. Courtesy of Iris Friedman. Photograph by John Manno.

The well-attended funeral of Charles Julianelli, aged fifty-four, was held at the Chapel of Saints Faith Hope and Charity, on Fifty-Eighth Street and Park Avenue, on the ground floor, with the open casket wake upstairs. Mourners wept deeply in collective grief. People said they hadn't even known that Charles was sick.

Mabel, in mourning, was unpretentious yet inspired in navy Norman Norell. Why look bad? For one thing Charles wouldn't have liked it. Her shoe was not Charles' favorite though; that would have been the Circe, any version of it. Mabel, always reserved, chose instead a demure navy crepe sandal with spike heel, an evening shoe nevertheless. She steadied herself against the back of a pew, flanked by family – Annette and Jack on one side and Onorata on the other. Janie, Johnny and Ona were cloaked under their grandmother's big black coat sleeves, whimpering like babies.

It seemed impossible, but everybody in their world came. After the closing rites they all piled upstairs to get a good look at him. And he was gorgeous, even in death. Someone said that Charles never had a bad day, and to look at him it appeared to be true. His face was serene, as if the mourners were eavesdropping on him, taking a moment to recline in the sun.

Mabel sat during the visitation period in a receiving pose across the room from the casket, plunged into a pompous crimson and black funeral parlor armchair that shrunk her dreadfully. The most one could see was her sad little face and head, bobbing to people she liked, bobbing to people she didn't like. It was Charles who taught her to like everyone for the good in them.

"It's barbaric!" wailed Phyllis through her handkerchief, flapping it at the gaping casket.

"It's uncivilized," Cousin Anne agreed, "but that's the Catholics for you."

"No, no, shush – it's what the family wanted," squeaked Mabel, pushing up to slap each woman across the knee with her navy suede-gloved hand, "and we're part of the family."

The two women solemnly agreed with her as the officiating priest presented himself. Mabel had soared once again with dignity, even though she couldn't get out of the chair, and took a long time, all knees and elbows to sit upright, which had them giggling.

"It's okay," said the priest, "laughter is what we're after. It's best to remember Charles and smile."

And so Mabel remembered, but that made it worse. Charles taught her how it felt to be on the arm of Cary Grant; he gave her the limelight and the credit for every shoe he designed and every construction he invented; he protected and defended her and gave her the confidence to be who she was;

he taught her to value the enormous beauty of Long Island, its land, its art and artists, and to value something even bigger – her own talent.

The crowd was so large that Mabel took home four guest registries, which were stacked for a very long time by her big picture window overlooking Carl Schultz Park and the East River. Mabel stayed at home, lonely and desolate. She was a piece of ribbon candy, just like *The New Yorker* said, and her wrapper was gone.

"Men's shoes – for women!"

"We had another shoe that Mabel did that I liked so much I put it in all different colors; it was a flat shoe and it had a little door knocker or drawer pull ornament on it. Then *Vogue* picked it up. And we sold tons of it. And then of course everybody knocked it off."

Gerald Blum, actor, innovator of fashion trends, former Executive Vice President of Lord & Taylor.

The office personnel kept Mabel in touch with what was happening, and the industry expected her to take some time off, but it wasn't as if she were sick, and Charles wasn't coming back, so she decided to go to lunch with Eva Rosencrans at B. Altman & Co.'s Charleston Gardens, where Scarlett O'Hara would have perked up at the glory of the magnolias, even though they were the wallpaper variety.

"What now, Mrs J.?" Vincent wailed, back at the office, with his wife Josephine and Leo, Sam, Eddie and Betty leaning over him to hear what she would say. They were all still employed by Mabel. Gone were her sister-in-law, Jeanne, who had moved to Ohio, and Phyllis who had married well.

Mabel paused a moment, and they thought she was going to cry. "We'll make a radical departure – isn't that what fashion wants?" she exclaimed. "'Held on by a string', my Aunt Tillie! We're not going to make strippy sandals anymore – we're going to make great big comfortable flat shoes, men's shoes – for women!"

Her widowhood was not going to be pathetic. She would hide her grief, as she always hid her deepest emotions. "Vincent, find Charles' fringe patterns! Leo, Sam, Eddie, get ready! You're making a thousand tassels. Josie, get the low-heel lasts! Betty, go to Macy's and pick up a big box of chocolate eggs! It's about to be spring!"

Mabel sat down at her peacock fan-back chair, sharpened her memory and a couple of number two pencils. She thought back to her light-weight perforated men's shoe, which was received with alarm on January 8th, 1950, when it was shown at the Costume Institute of the Metropolitan Museum of Art's Adam Through The Looking Glass exhibition, because Mabel had stated that shoe laces were a nuisance. It had been a riotous success just the same. "Let men have the works," Mabel said, "color and comfort." Applause came from two formidable fashion designers in the exhibition: Hattie Carnegie, who dressed her male model in an Eisenhower jacket and scarf of red, white and blue, and Lily Daché whose model wore a grey Spencer jacket trimmed in brown, and a cummerbund.

The other designers for the exhibition – Mabel was the only shoe designer – were Valentina, Clare Potter, Claire McCardell, milliner Sally Victor, Sophie Gimbel of Saks Fifth Avenue, and Leslie Morris of Bergdorf Goodman, Tina Leser, and Mrs Brooke Cadwallader.

Opposite: Raquel Welch wearing Julianelli Aladdin-inspired curled-toe thongs. *Vogue*, 1967. David Bailey/Condé Nast Archive; Copyright © Condé Nast Publications.

Polaire Weissman, executive director of The Costume Institute in 1950, suggested why women designers were chosen rather than men: '1. it seemed like a good idea; 2. men's clothes have always been designed by men; 3. women are mostly the deciding factor in what a man buys anyway.'

That was a long time ago, Mabel recalled, but fashion was all about refreshing the old, and it was customary for Mabel to look back to look forward. Vincent was a bit of a pushover and so were Leo, Sam and Eddie, and would do virtually anything she wanted. Mabel was a wonderful boss and soon had her little corporation humming again. Vincent was dragged into the search for Mabel's 1940s ornament designs, some with materials Charles sent her from Army camps in Virginia or Wyoming, and which Mabel handmade during the wartime years.

In the 1960s Mabel began a campaign for sleek little low-heeled pumps for daytime, or moccasins, Oxfords with kiltie-flaps (a fringe that looks like a Scottish kilt). Since she was always two seasons ahead of the garment industry, she had to anticipate what was coming next. Her evening shoes were now called slippers, but the word slipper was also a return to the 1940s. She loved the new lingo and went with it. She bared the shoe, pared it, and made it in a metallic braid t-strap, an Aladdin-inspired curled-toe thong or a silk, velvet and satin cocktail pump, with the most unusual ornaments, revised out of silver, brass, gilt, wood, and encrusted rhinestones.

The big difference was the small heel.

"Do women get to wear flats?" her friend, designer Chester Weinberg, asked Mabel in 1966.

A designer of above-the-knee dresses, often with uneven hems, Weinberg adored Mabel's taste.

"Right-o," said Mabel, modishly. And Chester Weinberg designed the little brown dress — asymmetrical, big-buttoned, in mocha linen — to pair with Mabel's drawer-pull ornament on an orange patent leather flat.

Mabel held lunch meetings in the Round Table Room at the Algonquin on West Forty-Fourth Street, near her office, and invited other shoe designers to attend: Herbert and Beth Levine, David Evins, and Silvia Fiorentina, Wanda Ferragamo, when in town, all of whom she admired, as well as fashion

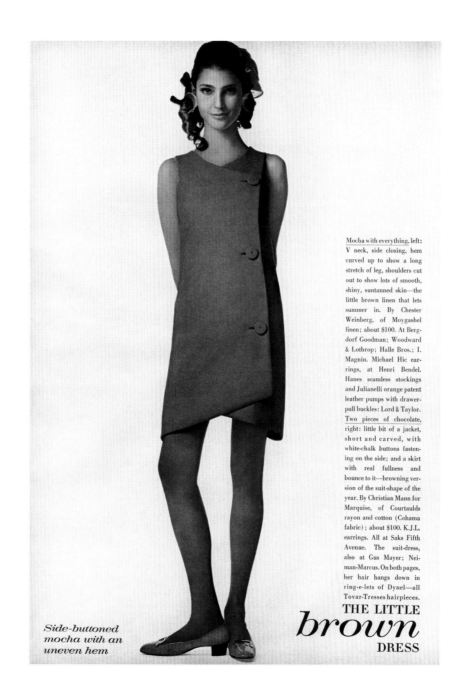

Mocha with everything, left: V neck, side closing, hem curved up to show a long stretch of leg, shoulders cut out to show lots of smooth, shiny, suntanned skin—the little brown linen that lets summer in. By Chester Weinberg, of Moygashel linen; about $100. At Bergdorf Goodman; Woodward & Lothrop; Halle Bros.; I. Magnin. Michael Hic earrings, at Henri Bendel. Hanes seamless stockings and Julianelli orange patent leather pumps with drawer-pull buckles: Lord & Taylor. Two pieces of chocolate, right: little bit of a jacket, short and carved, with white-chalk buttons fastening on the side; and a skirt with real fullness and bounce to it—browning version of the suit-shape of the year. By Christian Mann for Marquise, of Courtaulds rayon and cotton (Cohama fabric); about $100. K.J.L. earrings. All at Saks Fifth Avenue. The suit-dress, also at Gus Mayer; Neiman-Marcus. On both pages, her hair hangs down in ring-e-lets of Dynel—all Tovar-Tresses hairpieces.

THE LITTLE *brown* DRESS

Side-buttoned mocha with an uneven hem

designers, fashion magazine and newspaper editors, buyers and store managers whom she liked to join her on these occasions. The dress designers kept quiet, while the resolute shoe designers described next season's look.

It was a time of wonderful ornamentation but something else was brought into play – Mabel's knowledge of stockings, again from the wartime years. The rationing of silk in those days had led to the evolution of cotton stockings in a variety of textures, patterns and colors. Now the fabrics were synthetic. "The low pump must have a textured stocking, even for evening," she declared. Parrot-green fishnets went with an alabaster cut-out shoe set on a black wood heel; stretch nylon brown mini-pane checked leotards were paired with her gilt-buckled brown patent slipper; there was knitted wool in orange, yellow and pink, and white crochet. All the hosiery companies followed the shoes – Christian Dior, Roman Stripe, Hanes, Van Raalte, Beautiful Bryans, Lady Exeter, Ariadne, Mary Grey, Adler, Trimfit, Bewitching, and Hudson.

Mabel's ingenuity with stocking patterns was drawn from her experience in the 1940s, with wartime shortages and rationing of silk, when her efforts were to be creative with the only material she had – cotton – a material which led to the patterns and textures and colors that evolved from scarcity.

Mabel was inspired by the English and American country antiques which she had collected with Charles when she designed a drawer-pull ornament, and Lord & Taylor's favorite, her door-knocker ornament. Gerald Blum, the Lord & Taylor Salon shoe buyer at that time, who later became the Executive Vice President of Lord & Taylor, spoke to *Footwear News* about Mabel's low-heeled pump with her door-knocker ornament: "All the ladies in New York had to have them."

Many outfits went with this little flat: an Originala short safari suit or jacketed dress, with wide skirts paired with textured stockings from Roman Stripe or Christian Dior, and Samuel Robert's coats, as well as Chester Weinberg's little brown dress, worn with Hanes brown opaque stockings. Another shoe strongly promoted by Lord & Taylor was a low to medium heel pump with a bit buckle.

Lord & Taylor's Gerald Blum loved it so much that he ordered it in silk satin, suede, python and calf, brown, black, taupe and red.

Non-stop Legs, a Julianelli shoe plays with a textured stocking, *Vogue*, 1968. Art Kane/Condé Nast Archive; Copyright © Condé Nast Publications.

The fashion industry never felt timid concerning Mabel's vision, and never worried that she could miss the mark, because she never did. Everyone noticed that these new Julianelli shoes were a departure from Mabel's dainty pumps and sandals from earlier years; even when the toe was closed the pump still had an airy, feminine, open look. "Well, women's thinking does change, you know," was her reply.

Mabel did not have to search far for the new proportions to catch up with her shoes. Women had started wearing pants and short hemlines which were just right. It may have surprised her audience, but it did not surprise Mabel, that her ideas did not arise from imagination alone, but that Mabel's use of unusual ornamentation, textured stockings, with her design treatment, was a fashion three-way she launched in the 1940s.

Blum, while the Salon shoe buyer at Lord & Taylor, met Mabel in Europe for the leather shows. One aspect of Gerald Blum was remarkable, thought Mabel: he could set trends, not just sell them. He was marvelous at trend-setting. To him, Mabel was a true designer, one of the few. They taxied around Paris or Rome, looked in shoe store windows and lunched at Le Tour d'Argent. They would be excited by some fashion styles and appalled by others. It was understood that neither was committed to the current trend or what was predicted to be successful in the future. Mabel included Blum in her little get-togethers in her brownstone on East Eighty-Sixth Street and East End Avenue to which she moved in 1963.

In Paris, Mabel stayed at the Hôtel Plaza Athénée on Avenue Montaigne. Once, when they didn't have a room for her or the reservation had been mixed up, she sat in the lobby and did not move. Finally, after watching her for hours, the concierges found her some little room used for the employees of the hotel, and she was perfectly happy. She told her Cousin Iris, "I know who I am now and no one can throw me out of a hotel, especially not for Fashion Week!"

Unusual ornamentation was Mabel's gift and Lord & Taylor celebrated it. Bit buckle, Lord & Taylor, 1969. Lord & Taylor

The shoe must go on

At the end of the 1960s, Mabel stayed home and entertained only close friends. No more razzle-dazzle parties for seventy-five. She entertained with contained extravagance, a stoop's climb above street level, in her intimate rear receiving parlor, famous for its try-anything-in-here red wallpaper by Scalamandre. The floor covering was Stark, and Brunschwig & Fils covered the two English country armchairs, an English wrought iron bed, and a madness of throw pillows depicting various flora from the Cotswolds. Below this, in her garden-level dining room, Mabel used dinnerware from Dansk and flatware from Georg Jensen, or her best silverware if Brooks, Weinberg, Kasper, or Valentino were coming.

Her guests were her friends: Florence and Bob Eisner, Leon Turo, Eva Rosencrans, Roslyn Rosier and Roslyn's husband the doctor, Gerald Blum, her fashion designer friends, and always some contingent of contentious relatives.

Mabel knew people, but she was lonely. She could not have felt the certainty of an all consuming bereavement without living through it for the eight years since Charles' death. In doing so, she realized that, consciously or not, she had made a decision to spend the rest of her life tying up loose ends, seeing that her child would be provided for, and readying herself to join Charles in the grave.

Mabel kept Julianelli Inc. going, designed and traveled for the business, saw her daughter grow up, go to college and get married and she bought the brownstone across Eighty-Sixth Street from the apartment they had been living in when Charles died. Post Charles, she managed to discover new techniques for being sociable or fun-loving, even funny. But like replacement parts, these methods lacked something of the originals.

For years Mabel lunched in a succession of nearby department store spots with buyers, friends, and her daughter: Lord & Taylor's Bird Cage, B. Altman's Charleston Gardens, or Bonwit Teller's Mr Jennings, until one by one they closed. She liked to meet her daughter who had now grown up and insisted on being called Jane.

"Janie," Mabel said, "have a tuna melt."

Jane had been an amusing kid growing up, with loads of boyfriends and best friends. She loved her childhood and her home life, and gained confidence because she had many people to turn to – her mother, her cousins, Johnny and Ona, her mother's cousins, Steve, Iris and Anne, her grandma, and her old governess and friend, Miss McGowan. It was a good way to start out and Mabel provided that for her.

"Why always a tuna melt?" asked Jane.

"We didn't have it when I was growing up. No one ever thought about putting fish and cheese together. But it's delicious!" Mabel replied.

Mabel and Jane had managed to get through The Beatles, Woodstock and Women's Liberation, even with the conflicts of two generations, and came out the other end as friends. She leaned on Jane a bit for company, but that was all right because Mabel was always fun. Mabel missed her department store haunts when they closed. She missed her sister-in-law Annette who moved to Albany, and Jeanne who moved to Ohio. Luigi Giulianelli had died. She missed her buddy, Gerald Blum, who was still at Lord & Taylor, but wasn't in the shoe department, even though she saw him in the summer and sometimes on weekends in Long Island, where he had bought a house, one town over.

A revelation, one weekend morning

Mabel returned for a summer weekend to Rose Cottage with difficulty. Friends had moved and friends had died. She went with Jane as much as her daughter's social life would permit. They would pack up Mabel's orange-red Dodge Dart that her deal-maker brother Ben found for her, leave the parking garage on Seventy-Ninth Street around 5 pm on Friday, and not get back to the city until 8 pm on Sunday.

Vincent, with his wife, Josie, drove Onorata, now in her eighties, out to be with them. On Sunday they went to the A & P to get the papers and ant traps. Or they went to the Candy Kitchen luncheonette. Vincent and Josie shared strawberry ice cream; while Mabel had her old faithful, maple walnut, and Grandma and Jane chose butter pecan. Sometimes Mabel's first cousins, Anne Robinson and the younger ones, Steve Friedman and his pretty wife, Iris came for a weekend and they ate ice cream too.

Weekends were about ice cream. It was that uncomplicated. Through her bouts of introversion, what she called her 'nerves', which left her quite exhausted, Mabel found the simplest activities at Rose Cottage to be the best. She did everything a fine country woman would do – she left out tuna fish for the wild cats, while wondering if the bulging wild turkeys hadn't eaten it instead, she went about the house and made note of a leak in the roof, cut a few roses, ate a buttered roll from the Sagg Store, and read Harold Robbins.

It was a tight house, though – no drafts, no leaks, the normal squeaks when the wind blew, with indications all over it of having been, throughout a century, well taken care of. So she made peace with it, and it became her hiding place, where she withdrew from a New York City which was getting younger by the minute.

One weekend morning there was a knock on the kitchen door. It seemed Lucia Wilcox had come to pay a call. On her own turf, Mabel sized up the small, dark woman, who was seven years her senior. Lucia had gray hair now, but was still beautiful.

"Mabel had a certain level of taste. She knew good food. She had traveled through Europe many times, probably, a minimum of four times a year, and she ate at the best restaurants wherever she was.

When we'd come out to Long Island on a Saturday morning, we would stop off the highway at Howard Johnson's. Mabel always ordered her coffee hot, and her pancakes 'thin and brown'. She was even discerning in Howard Johnson's. Did she expect the quality of a five star restaurant in Europe at Howard Johnson? Well, she expected her pancakes thin and brown. And she got them that way. It was one of the big trends she started, at least with the family."

Iris Friedman, wife of Steve Friedman, Mabel's first cousin.

Lucia was making a condolence call. There had been a card sent directly after Charles' death, but coming in person had taken many years to do.

From Charles' first meeting with the artist Lucia, and through all their intense, artistic episodes painting together, observing together, Charles had felt his professional life decline and fall, as he indulged in the pleasurable act of painting once more. Mabel had always known this. But even with this pleasure, his loyalty as Mabel's husband, to which so many years had been dedicated for better or for worse, never once faltered. This fact Mabel did not know for sure.

Only Lucia knew it, and told Mabel directly that morning.

As Lucia left across the yard, Mabel remembered back to when Charles was coming home from the Wilcox place, so happy and with a longing, which, time after time, Mabel dreaded. Lucia made her aware for the first time that morning that his joy and longing were for his painting and Lucia's only part in it had been to give him the outlet to pursue it. To know that Charles had never betrayed her brought Mabel tears of joy; and that it had been told to her by none other than her suspected rival, Lucia, brought tears of remorse.

On her flight to Los Angeles, one of the Julianellis' favorite cities, where they had traveled together to make many public appearances, Mabel was a perfect *tour-de-force* in Kasper's black three-button blazer and skirt, a pink handbag, and on her feet, her Julianelli signature tuxedo low-heels in black patent leather with a black grosgrain bow and mini door-knocker ornament.

The descending plane, breaking through the horizon, aimed her thoughts toward L.A., its movie stars – an obsession of her childhood – movie lots, movie studios, movie premieres – life California style. Yet nothing could make her feel more like a New Yorker.

Mabel felt Charles' absence. For a woman who had learned the value of fine things, Mabel was hopeless with money. She knew how to make it; she knew how to spend it. Mabel was always overly generous to those she loved, and besides, saving was a responsibility she had never had to think of, since Charles handled the finances and had left her very comfortable, with both real estate and money in the bank.

Top left: Cousin Iris Friedman vacationing
in Coeur d'Alene, Idaho, 1987.
Bottom left: Mabel Julianelli and Cousin
Steve Friedman in East Hampton, 1989.
Right: Mabel and Jane share Christmas day,
opening presents, 1980.

However, nine years after Charles' death, it was another story. For the task of paying her bills, Mabel thought she might hire one of the wholesome-looking people at the Seventy-Ninth Street branch of Chemical Bank, and before long there were monthly visits from a drab, unpleasant clerk, writing out checks while sitting apprehensively on an armchair, upholstered in plush Brunschwig & Fils green damask. The man soon quit, croaking all the way out the door that balancing Mabel's checkbook was a fate worse than death.

One night the heat went off. Did Mabel pay the electric bill, she wondered, or was the boiler down? And where was the boiler? Mabel would not call anyone and would not leave her house. She sat in her living room wearing her Donald Brooks Stone Marten coat until the heat came on.

It was not until then that Mabel remembered Papa Winkel, in one of his cheerier moods, warning her that a woman was always more likely to become destitute than a man. But she tried not to see it that way. She had been too busy working her whole life to oversimplify human beings the way Papa Winkel did.

She had a notion that if she bought one good dress and one good suit, á la Norman Norell's advice, then she wouldn't need any others. However, her friends were too talented and too great to ignore – her friends being Donald Brooks, Kasper, Bill Blass, Geoffrey Beene, and Chester Weinberg – so off she went to their Seventh Avenue showrooms on a Saturday morning, where nothing came cheap, even wholesale. She bought from them, and inevitably took somebody to the Stage Deli for lunch.

Losing a most precious thing

The 1960s had offered up many opportunities to make public appearances to enhance her business, and Mabel thought that in the 1970s she would make even more public appearances, and doing this would surely save the day.

Bullock's Wilshire was truly a California store, with a glamorous shoe salon and lots of junior buyers waiting to tell Mabel how she inspired them. It was a very important showing. In the late 1960s, the silk crepe evening trousers, velvet gowns, little daytime linen dresses, and short dressy suits craved the Julianelli robust low-heeled buckled pump, as did the knitted, textured stockings and the jeweled leotards that accessorized them. A chunky, clunky fashion was refined under Mabel's ladylike pencil. She could put the lady in anything. The public always knew it was a Julianelli.

But now, in the early 1970s, Mabel refined the toe, raised the heel, dressed the pump or laced it for day and evening, for gowns or trousers, hot pants or peasant dresses. These were the new arrivals at Bullock's Wilshire, Cardinale, Himelhoch's, Lord & Taylor, Bonwit Teller and Saks Fifth Avenue.

The shoe salon at Bullock's burst with a tremendous welcome sign, clanking magnificently on its chain over Mabel. She was seated in a replica of the fan-back chair she had in her office, a detail which someone thought was clever. An assortment of merchandise managers, buyers and junior buyers edged in closer. Someone in that group had been to her office and seen her chair, but she didn't know who, and felt slightly exposed. She sat there clutching her blazer, her handbag and her knees. If she were made of squeezable plastic she couldn't have looked more like a wind-up doll, especially with the sign overhead which she imagined read: 'Wind her up and she'll talk about shoes,' but actually read, 'Mabel Julianelli is here today.'

This public appearance felt like all the rest, a conspicuous display of Mabel-without-Charles. At least Bullock's had not removed all reference to Charles, as evidenced by a tiny copy line at the very bottom of the sign that read, 'By the *people* who never forgot about pretty shoes.'

In 1973, sitting in her own wicker fan-back chair in her office, sketching at her desk with the orange and aqua-colored markers she used at that time, Mabel was informed by Betty, now somewhat decrepit but still Boop-ish, that a man from Andrew Geller Inc. was on the phone. A call from a busy, successful shoe firm was always welcome, Mabel thought, picking up the phone, tears filling her

"Mabel had enormous drive and enormous talent. Charles executed her designs. He made them real. We used to sit in the Plaza Athénée and she would make little sketches, and lo-and-behold, Charles made it happen. She missed him terribly. She wouldn't go to the Ritz in Paris anymore because that's where they stayed. She wouldn't live in the apartment that she had on East End Avenue because they lived there. That's when she bought the brownstone.

As much as Mabel loved the memory of Charles she did not like to be in the places that brought up the fact that he wasn't there anymore. She made major changes in her life, bought a house, would not stay in a hotel that knew her for years. She didn't think she could do it without him."

Phyllis Footer, former Vice President of Schwartz & Benjamin.

Opposite: Three-toned metallic ankle strap with raised back, heel: 3⅜ inches, 1970. Photograph by John Manno.

Mabel, in Oscar de la Renta, on her daughter's
wedding day, 1971. Photograph by Geoffry Fried.

Slim heel ankle-tie sandal, a Julianelli classic from the '60s, which was brought back by ballroom dancers, heel: 3½ inches, late 1970. Photograph by John Manno.

Patent leather naked sandal that twists on vamp, heel: 3½ inches, 1980. Photograph by John Manno.

eyes as she anticipated some kind of condolence, even after all these years. It started predictably with the heavy, unfamiliar voice stating how deeply they all missed Charles.

The night before, Mabel went about collecting photographs and spreading them on her bed, in her second-floor master bedroom that overlooked Eighty-Sixth Street and a slice of Carl Schultz Park. Her daughter was already married, the reception held at the Algonquin, in the Oak Room, where Mabel once hosted luncheons for fashion people in the 1960s.

In a few of the wedding photographs Jane posed and played, and flaunted her beautiful white lace dress with her bridesmaids in blue and red gingham – Kasper all the way. In another photograph, Mabel weaved between guest tables, looking ravishing in floor-length Oscar de la Renta, drifting into sugary conversations about the lovely reception, the lovely newlyweds, and the lovely Oak Room. Even the industry people on her guest list behaved themselves and gave up fashion chatter for the reception. She did not divulge for one moment the rising storm of panicky thoughts going on in her mind.

Mabel never spoke of it, but a few weeks before, on the day she had bought the Oscar de la Renta gown, she had been to a closing at her attorney's office to sell the Terbell Lane property on Hook Pond; it was the jewel in Charles' portfolio, the property which her husband purchased just to be romantic. The sale had produced a paltry succession of dollar bills, but it paid for the wedding. There were other properties she sold. When no property was left except Rose Cottage, Mabel turned to something else.

On hearing the offer of the Andrew Geller representative on the phone, the red and aqua markers slipped from Mabel's fingers and she had a sudden urge to go to a place where she always felt comforted. She invited Cousin Anne and Cousin Iris to join her. By the time she would cab it back to her office from Seventy-Ninth Street, her mind was made up.

"Why would you sell your trade name to Andrew Geller?" asked young Cousin Iris, during the butterscotch sundae at Schrafft's.

"It's a desperate day," said Mabel, "but perhaps I am attracted to the suggestion of money."

Above: Town shoe with braid, Lord & Taylor, 1971. Lord & Taylor.
Opposite: Suggestive of a Mabel Winkel & Co. innovation – her 1940 sport shoe, the Oxford flat is a return to Mabel's man-tailored look, single-tie, high vamp, heel, 1 inch, 1970. Photograph by John Manno.

Opposite: Mabel said, "Stay away from extremes in shoe styles which will keep your feet healthier – and you happier." Walking moccasin with tassel, mid heel: 2¼ inches, 1970. Photograph by John Manno.

This page: Chester Weinberg loved this shoe in the '60s with his short dresses because it was low but ladylike. This is the '70s tassel kiltie 'moc', heel: 1 inch. Courtesy of Phoebe Dunst. Photograph by John Manno.

She went to Altman's with the intention of having her hair dyed the bombshell blond that went over so big at the Barberry Room, thirty years before, but it wasn't her anymore. She'd miss the comfortable downtown lunchrooms in Altman's or Lord & Taylor if she worked for Andrew Geller Inc. Andrew Geller Inc. was uptown, near the Chock full o'Nuts lunch counter. Of course, Chock full o'Nuts had a great cream cheese on raisin bread sandwich, but what it did not have were the uncomfortable tray tables welded to their chairs at the Bird Cage, where you tried to squeeze into one and could only converse with the person to your right. And it most certainly did not have the wallpaper Magnolias of the Charleston Gardens. These places were still open but on their last leg. So much of the charm of New York was becoming obsolete.

Julianelli under Andrew Geller Inc. continued to carry out collections which were referred to as 'timeless feminine footwear', and Mabel's name alone appeared in many ads during the early 1970s. However, soon the ads were changed to read: 'By Mabel Julianelli for the Julianelli line of Andrew Geller'. She had been purchased, and it was a state of affairs she grew to loathe.

Mabel designed high, thick-heeled t-straps, slings and dress moccasins, and smooth caramel-colored leather boots, with a narrow leg and slender toe, which were bought by Bullock's Wilshire. Lord & Taylor featured her braiding and her russet monk-strap. For Halle's and Neiman-Marcus she designed her single-tie Oxford flats, and her kiltie-flap Oxfords were for Bonwit Teller and Sakowitz. Mabel designed a metallic-edged black pump for Zandra Rhodes' silk jacquard dress, and a bare high-heeled sandal for Ralph Lauren's pinstripe pant suit. She brought back the slender toe ghillie in luggage-tan because she sensed that ribbed tights were coming around again, and the metallic open low heels because Mabel predicted that low heels for evening were coming back as well.

Mabel traveled for Andrew Geller Inc., to their factory in Italy. Shoe making was altogether different now. Bench-making was a forgotten art, the kind of bench-made or hand-made shoes which Charles, Leo, Sam, Eddie and Vincent once constructed. With a bang like a shotgun, the die-cut machine dropped on the leather and a pattern was stamped.

When she traveled in the United States, Mabel was greeted by buyers and customers who knew who she was and what her name stood for. Her tailored tuxedo flat was shown in black patent or suede with a grosgrain bow. At the other end of the spectrum, because she worked best when sparring with two opposite looks, she revised her 'naked' sandal and it was shown with Halston's tissue-sheer body shaper. All her 'naked' sandals across the years had caused people's eyes to pop out, because of the degree to which their diaphanous strips of leather had reached beyond delicacy.

Opposite: Mabel once said, "I think of Hepburn and I think, put a kiltie over that vamp!" Katharine Hepburn met Mabel Julianelli at the March of Dimes fashion show in 1948. Monk-strap kiltie, heel: 2¾ inch, 1970. Photograph by John Manno.

Opposite: The tuxedo pump with oversized grosgrain bow and tapered toe. Geoffrey Beene pared this pump with his tailored suits, heel: 1 inch, 1980. Photograph by John Manno.

In August 1977, an ad appeared in the *Los Angeles Times*, for Bullock's Wilshire, announcing her arrival on Thursday at the Wilshire Blvd. store, Friday at the Newport store and Saturday at Woodland Hills. She was traveling as she had done as a young woman. The ad featured Mabel's new stack heels, moccasins and boots,

'all from the lady who's built a reputation by doing one thing for years and doing it very well indeed.'

Another ad in a Californian newspaper, the *Sunday Peninsula Herald,* announced her personal appearance at Cardinale Fine Shoes, and read: 'To step out in shoes by Mabel Julianelli is to wear with pride the most feminine footwear of positive elegance.'

By the next week she was in the Designer Shoes department at Bonwit Teller in New York, giving a special course in Western civilization with her redefined, urbane Julianelli boots.

In 1980, Mabel's contract with Andrew Geller Inc. terminated, and Mabel left, but her precious Julianelli name stayed behind. It was only then that she could admit, saddened without her name, without Charles' name, that her business dealings with Andrew Geller Inc. had been a mistake. The Julianelli brand was carried on for a limited time, but it would never be Mabel's again.

"It's all gone," said Mabel, "and my ambition with it."

"You were always so ambitious," said Cousin Anne.

Once interviewed by fashion historian and journalist June Weir, who was, in 1980, an editor at *Vogue*, Mabel was quoted, in *Vogue's* View, on the subject of her biggest influence: 'Ambition! I wanted to be a success. I wanted to develop my own ideas. I tried to be innovative with shoes.'

She was seventy-three.

Opposite: High heel leather boot, 1978.
As seen in US *Harper's Bazaar.*
Bottom left: High heel day pump, 1978.
As seen in US *Harper's Bazaar.*
Bottom right: High heel ankle-strap, 1973.
As seen in US *Harper's Bazaar.*

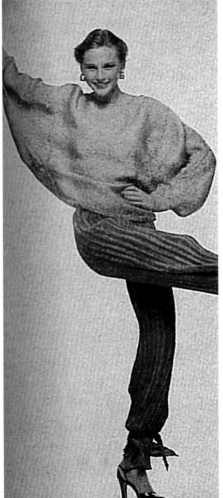

Part Three:
Mabel Without Julianelli

Opposite: Shoe Boxes with Mabel Julianelli's signature, sweeping across in gold, 1940-1970. Photograph by John Manno.

232

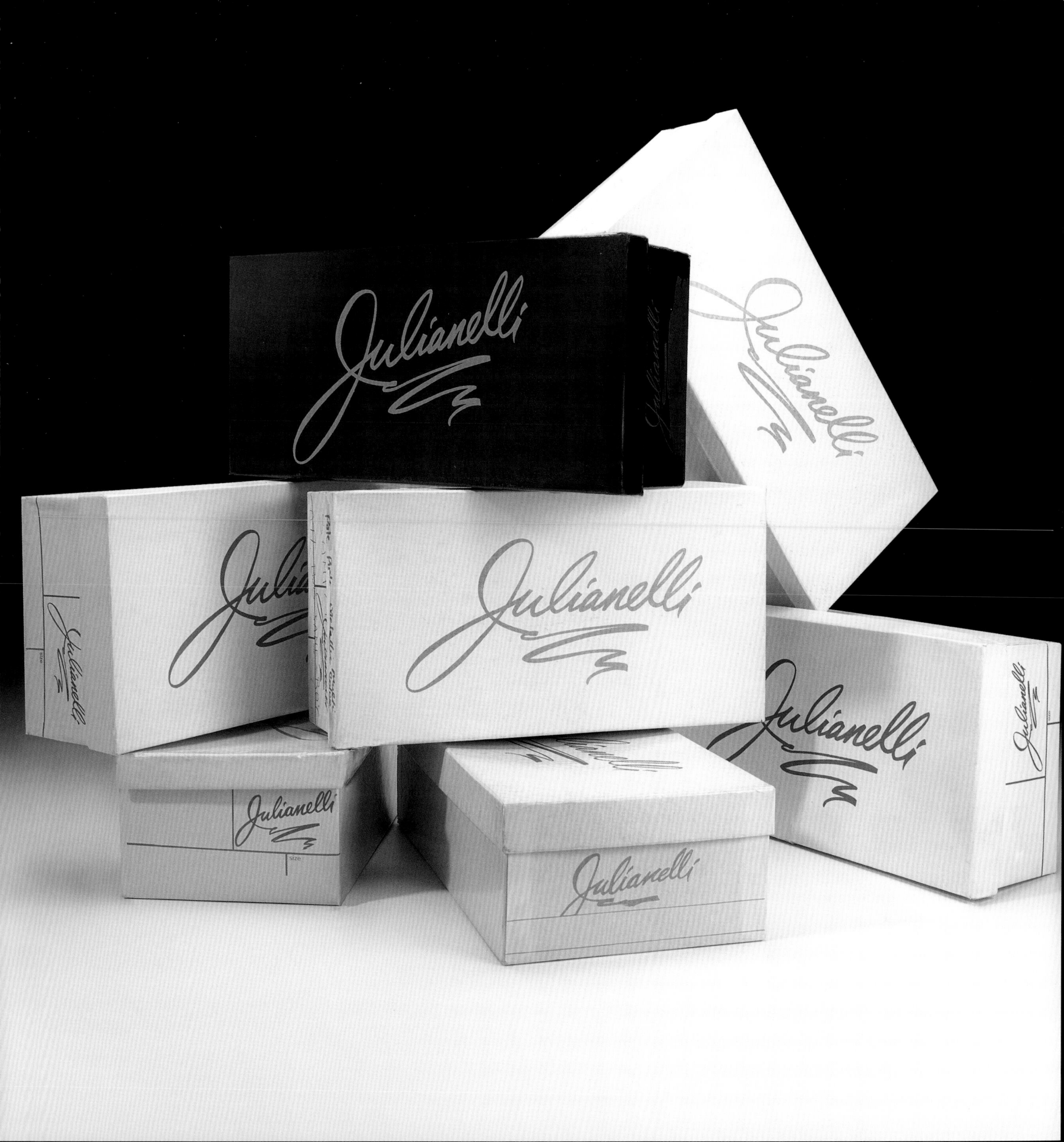
Julianelli

Mabel without Julianelli

Mabel resolved to be a happy old lady, and through the 1980s and the early1990s, put her mind to it, like taking up dieting or needlepoint. However, when Mabel looked back, it nearly killed her – from young darling to obscure old lady in sixty speedy years. It was unbelievable, and what was just as unbelievable was that she had read nine Harold Robbins books and actually enjoyed wearing sweatpants. Informality called her, but she was always elegant.

The family could only remember Mabel having one pair of dress pants that she had made up in Europe. They were from her favorite European designer, Valentino. But she very rarely wore them. Pongee silk skirts with matching blouses, shift dresses in heavy cotton, sweaters, and tweed skirts made up her preferred dress code. Though loyal to her designer friends, from time to time she picked up something vintage.

Mabel had redecorated her brownstone in the City three times. Having outlived her friend Roslyn Rosier, the decorator, she did it once on her own. She thought Roslyn would approve. Having outlived her mother-in-law, Mabel grew tomatoes, basil and chives at Rose Cottage, and served Jewish spaghetti with the tiny onion rolls from William Greenberg. She thought Onorata would approve.

Having outlived her husband, her father, father-in-law, sister-in-law Annette, sister Helen, her brothers, her cousin Anne, Vincent and Josie, and every one of her men, she deeply valued her life and the treasures it had to draw on, the most humbling of these being good times, laughter, her daughter, and the devotion of a kind-hearted man.

Some days, Mabel implored the years to talk back to her, to reveal what she could have done differently to prevent Charles' untimely death and the sale of her trade name. But the answers never came.

In retrospect, Mabel could have thrown one of her great parties, announced that she was retiring, with the Julianelli name still hers, and

the fashion industry would have implored her to consult, lecture, and design a line of clothes, or perfume, or kitchen gadgets.

Now she simply wished to spend as much time as was left being where Charles once was and doing the things he once liked to do.

For sixty years Mabel had lived and worked among the most stimulating and diverse people in New York: designers, artists, decorators, inventors, editors, and artisans. Besides that, her home had been an integration of cultures. How lucky she was to have been a part of it during the brief twenty-two years she was Mrs Charles Julianelli.

One evening, as dinner from the Sagg Store of roasted chicken and corn pudding stuffed her family with contentment, Mabel had one eye on the television. When the family got together it was usually an uproarious time, but laughter bounced off Mabel as she watched a newscast in which an Indian elephant, wandering out of its protected habitat, had been tortured and maimed by poachers with a four-hundred bore rifle, and left to die, northeast of New Delhi. Forestry officials reported that the Ganesha, named after the Hindu deity, had been too old to fight back.

Ah yes, Mabel remembered the Balaganapati, not by name, but by the feeling of being so incredibly lifted, while riding the majestic and venerable elephant, at a time back in 1959, when elephants were worshipped and revered.

Mabel still had her hair done, her old reddish brown, and still put herself together neatly in a dirndl skirt and nubby sweater, scarf at the neck, a lined raincoat and low-heeled pumps.

"I lost my name," she said to Jane one day.

"You'll get your name back, Mom."

Mabel felt safe at Rose Cottage, the place she had once called the boondocks. It lacked the intensity of the City, but was a comfort to its artists and to all who lived there, with its roaring spaces of ocean, fields, forest and sky. Mabel went often and finally fixed the leaky roof. Among her family there was talk of leasing for her a little shop in one of the villages, where she could sell something crazy, like shoes. Other accessories would be on hand; Mabel and Jane would buy, Cousin Iris would sell, Cousin Anne would point, and Cousin Steve would read the newspaper and shake his head. It was a lovely thought, but after all this time, Mabel could hear Charles telling her to slow down and enjoy her elder years, something he never got to do. So Mabel took up drawing portraits, perhaps in remembrance of Charles, her medium, charcoal. She drew her daughter, her cousins, the trees, birds, rabbits, the ocean, but no other shoe ever came out of her.

When she was eighty, Mabel refused a big birthday party in September and said she'd wait for Christmas. Christmas was always spent in New York. Mabel, up in her bedroom, wrapped gloves, scarves and sweaters in brown and white striped boxes, tied with brown ribbon from Bendel's. There was a Christmas tree decorated with colored glass ornaments she saved through the years, and candles, especially a favorite small white Christmas tree candle with rhinestones stuck on by pins. Dinner was served at 3pm, after that the presents were opened. Mabel loved Christmas because Charles loved it. Each year, Mabel sat ornamentally in her favorite of the two living room armchairs, and would rest her Eggnog on a curio cabinet in-between.

Guests sprawled out on the carpet in front of a white marble-top coffee table, weighed down by a glass decanter of tree ornaments; others would sit on her sofa, Chester Weinberg's favorite, for which he chose the bronze-colored velvet upholstery fabric. Every time someone new came to Mabel's house, its sparkle shone in their eyes, catching the edge of a brass mirror frame, or gilded candelabra, or the Chinoiserie compositions painted by P. C. Canot.

On Christmas Day, 1980, Jane reminded Mabel of the time around 1964 when Mabel was on a business trip and had just made it home late one Christmas Eve to find no tree, and no prospect of a tree. Jane recounted that on the following morning, Christmas morning, she had told her daughter and Jane's visiting cousins to go up the street. Somebody, Mabel was certain, would discard unwanted Christmas tree branches.

They found one by the trash of an apartment building close by, one sweet-smelling crooked Balsam branch. Mabel covered it with gift-wrap bows. And, in the splendor of her living room, the branch fit beautifully. She was so good at ornamentation. That was Mabel.

Mabel and Charles stepped out for the evening. Dancing strippy mule, 1956. As seen in US *Harper's Bazaar.*

Mabel Julianelli died of heart failure on December 2nd, 1994. She would have wanted to be remembered living life to the fullest, with Charles by her side.

Index